The Country UNDERTAKER

Reminiscences of a bush life

JIM EAMES

ALLEN&UNWIN

To my mother, who bore it all
with such grace and resilience

First published in 2005

Copyright © Jim Eames 2005

Allen & Unwin
83 Alexander Street
Crows Nest NSW 2065 Australia
Phone: (61 2) 8425 0100
Fax: (61 2) 9906 2218
E-mail: info@allenandunwin.com
Web: www.allenandunwin.com

National Library of Australia
Cataloguing-in-Publication entry:

Eames, Jim, 1939– .
The country undertaker: reminiscences of bush life.

1st ed.
ISBN 1 74114 580 5.

1. Eames, Mick. 2. Undertakers and undertaking – Australia.
I. Title.

363.750994

Set in 11.6/16 pt Berling by Midland Typesetters, Maryborough, Victoria
Printed by Griffin Press, South Australia

10 9 8 7 6 5 4 3 2 1

Contents

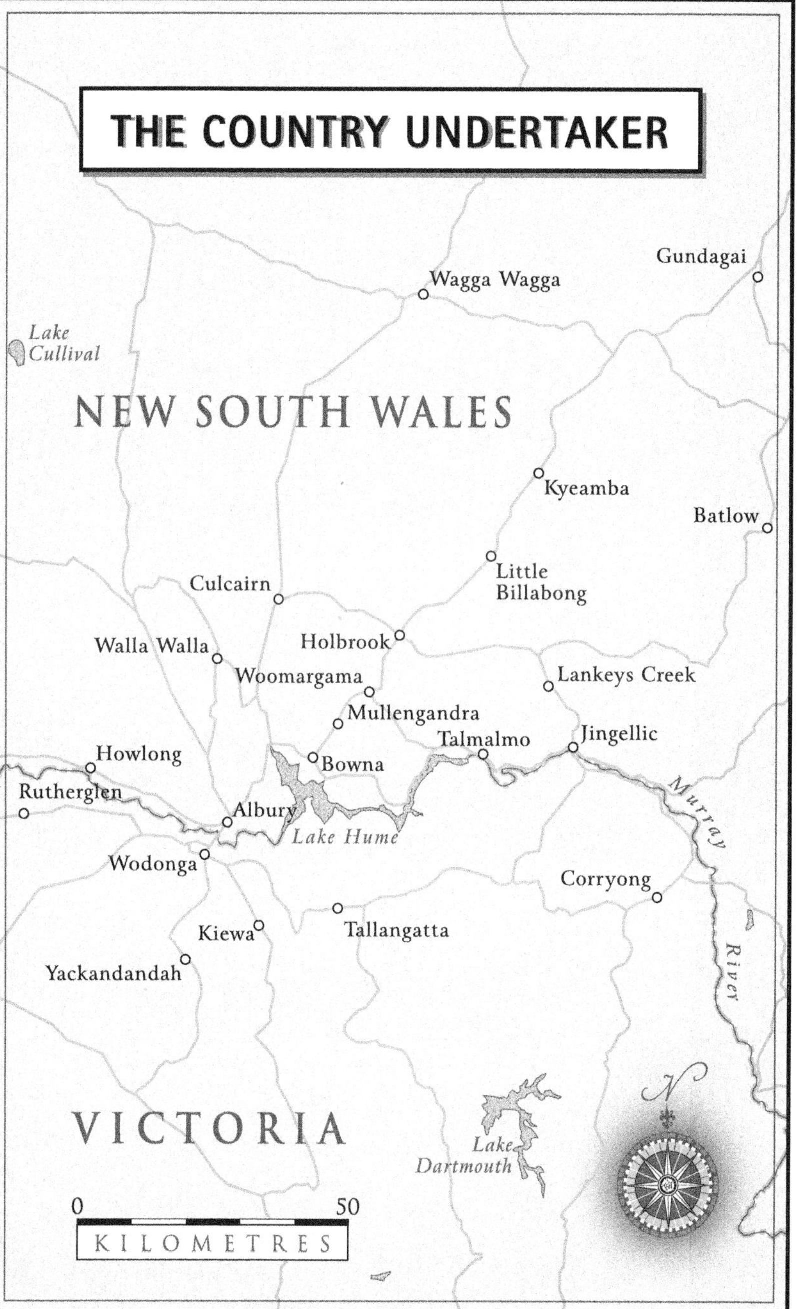

THE COUNTRY UNDERTAKER
Gundagai
Wagga Wagga
Lake Cullival
NEW SOUTH WALES
Kyeamba
Batlow
Little Billabong
Culcairn
Walla Walla
Holbrook
Woomargama
Lankeys Creek
Mullengandra
Talmalmo
Jingellic
Howlong
Bowna
Rutherglen
Albury
Lake Hume
Murray
Wodonga
Corryong
Kiewa
Tallangatta
River
Yackandandah
VICTORIA
Lake Dartmouth
N
0
50
KILOMETRES

In at the deep end

I know it might sound odd when you're talking about a dead person and grieving relatives, but you always want your first funeral to be a resounding success. Particularly if you're a small town country undertaker.

Not too big, just the reverend and a handful of mourners, a brief church service, a bit of a yarn on the footpath outside the church before maybe two or three of the mourners follow the hearse to the cemetery. An ideal practice run, really.

But things didn't work out that way for my father and here we were on a fine, sunny afternoon with a 1929 Essex hearse parked outside a church not only full of relatives and friends but overflowing with a group of unrelated people who had gathered to see off the patriarch of one of the district's landed gentry from out the Culcairn Road.

Here was my father, the brand new country undertaker, thrown in at the deep end of a funeral at least three times larger than he would have liked and probably the main reason I was sitting in the passenger's seat of the Essex, wearing long pants, the only white shirt I owned and one of my father's dark ties. He was convinced if you were operating a funeral business in a rich Riverina town like Holbrook, you needed a second person sitting in the hearse to put on a bit of a show.

I always thought the credit for that idea belonged to his long-time drinking mate Bill Lester, who ran Lester and Sons Funeral Directors in Albury. But my mother swore the motivation for having two people in the front came from my dad's first boss in Holbrook, Nace Kane, who insisted it looked better to have more live people in a hearse than dead ones. I had to admit this was more the type of logic which would have appealed to my father.

Not that sitting in the front seat was to be my only role. Because of his nervousness about the Essex and her poor record in the starting department, my father had developed a schedule designed to ensure everything was ready to roll precisely on time. Before he left to position himself, on this particular day, in the doorway of the church fifty yards away, his instructions were explicit.

'Don't take your eyes off me,' he said. 'The minute you see me leave the doorway with the casket and walk towards you, move across behind the wheel and be ready to kick the starter. I want her running as soon as the coffin slides in.'

Then he was gone. I soon found that keeping an eye on my father in these circumstances was easier said than done, mainly because he wasn't a tall man and his shock of dark hair kept disappearing behind the flow of people, as mourners moved up and down the steps outside the Catholic church doorway trying to get a better view of the proceedings.

It might too have been that day when I realised for the first time the reason men of the cloth like big funerals. They have a captive audience maybe three times the size of their normal Sunday services so they're not going to let an opportunity like this pass them by, and anyway, at a funeral it's not quite as easy for some of those down the back to slip out for a smoke in the middle of it all.

The murmur of voices from inside the church stopped suddenly, the crowd on the steps parted and there appeared my father, several paces in front of the four men bearing the casket. I slid across behind the steering wheel.

There was a moment of panic when I lost sight of him again as he came down the path and disappeared out of sight towards the back of the hearse, but then relief as I heard the shuffle of feet from behind, followed by a squeaking sound as the two rear doors of the hearse were swung open. That was the signal and I leaned forward and jammed my foot down hard on the rusty metal starting pedal which protruded from a hole in the wooden floorboards.

For about three seconds there was a high pitched whirring noise followed by a slow groaning sound from under the bonnet which gradually started to slow down, like the noise from one of those old 78 record players when the handle needs another turn. Then silence. The battery was flat. Having no idea what to do I just sat there, still nervously gripping the steering wheel with sweaty hands.

The next instant I was startled by my father's face appearing at the window alongside me. 'Quick, pass me the crank handle.' I could see by the colour of his cheeks that his blood pressure was up.

'When it fires, move that fuel mixture lever up slowly,' he continued, pointing to a six-inch long metal rod on top of the steering wheel, as he raced around to the front of the Essex, to be followed by a brief clank of metal upon metal as the crank handle was rammed home. At every turn of the handle his head would appear briefly above the radiator, his features now a vivid red, doubtless due in large part to the exertion—but probably more because of the fact that fifty or so of the deceased's grieving relatives and friends were now standing around waiting for the next move, not sure whether they should offer to give the Essex a push or get into their own cars and head for the cemetery in the hope that the hearse would follow them within a reasonable time.

Just as it seemed all was lost there was a loud report, a puff of smoke from somewhere under the bonnet and the old Essex burst into life. I hardly had time to push the lever upward when, all pretext of dignity now abandoned, Dad was back beside the driver's side door. I moved back to the passenger's seat. There was a clatter of metal upon wood as he threw the crank handle onto the floor in the front, a thud as the back doors were shut, then Dad was into the driver's seat and we were away, leaving the mourners to wander off towards their own transport, doubtless a little relieved they wouldn't have to push the old girl in the 24-degree heat.

Thus was the pattern established and the first assignment for Mick Eames, country undertaker, was off to a somewhat shaky start.

1

A colourful mob

I often wondered what qualifications you required to be a country undertaker because nothing in my father's past seemed to point in that direction. In fact I doubt whether anyone who knew my father would have expected him to end up spending a considerable amount of his life burying people. I also doubt it figured anywhere in his friendship with Bill Lester, of Lester and Sons Funeral Directors, as their relationship seemed to revolve more around a group of mates who all drank at McLennan's Terminus Hotel in Albury, my father's favourite watering hole. Sure, if any of the Eameses died it was Bill Lester who buried them. But apart from that nothing else in Dad's family background seemed to point to it.

My father was one of nine boys, no girls, and in the Eames family no one seemed to show any interest in anything beyond Australian Rules football, motor cars and, in the case of my father and several of his brothers, drinking. And as far as football was concerned it was hard to avoid the Eames name around Albury or Wodonga, as two of the brothers, Jack and Tom, made it to the Holy Grail of Australian Rules: they played for Richmond in the Victorian Football League, a feat their siblings considered somehow lifted their own reputation in the local team competition.

Shrewdly, my father could often be heard to say that he and his brothers inherited their talents from their father, George Eames senior. I had no memory of my grandfather, but the one photograph we had above our loungeroom fireplace in Townsend Street, Albury, showed a tall, well-built man with a round face, wearing a white open-neck shirt and dark trousers held up by braces. The photograph had been taken in the paddock which backed onto their house at the very bottom end of Townsend Street. It showed him anchoring one end of his brood of nine sons, all of whom stood sullenly looking at the camera, leaving little doubt they didn't want to be there. Alongside him was my grandmother Johanna, shorter, but more thickset, stooped slightly forward as if the responsibility of rearing nine boys had already taken its toll on her frame. Her hair parted oddly in the middle, and a large nose dominated her facial features. She was dressed in a dark, three-quarter length, one-piece smock buttoned up the middle which was short enough to show thick, very bandy legs.

The boys bobbed along to her right in a messy, uneven line as if somebody had decided they would be photo-graphed according to age rather than height. This meant the eldest, Dave, although one of the shortest, stood alongside his parents, the tallest ones, Sid and Tom, stood next to him then it went down to my father, up again to George junior and tailed off to the four youngest: Jack, Jeff, Frank and Phil, the last one barefoot and still in short pants. The only physical features they had in common were their ears—all were big and tended to protrude almost at right angles—and their mother's nose.

Dad never spoke much about his father, but I picked up impressions in other ways. My mother told me George senior was an old-fashioned Catholic who read a lot and held firm views on social justice, leaning towards the belief that since the wealth of the country was so obviously in the hands of the few, the only recourse for the worker was to band together and do what he could to look after himself and his mates. Usually when she got to this point in the story, my mother would allude, now almost in a quasi-conspiratorial whisper, to his leadership of some sort of clan where secret meetings were held and pamphlets distributed. She seemed vague on the contents of the pamphlets, except to hint they were dangerous and if you were caught with such literature you could be sent to jail. You could tell from the way she said it that if she'd personally ever been handed one she'd have dropped it like a hand grenade, as it wasn't the sort of thing a somewhat shy, self-conscious woman wanted anything to do with. I think she got some of the story from her own father who didn't like George Eames senior much, calling him a 'commo' because of the meetings and the pamphlets (which, it turned out, were about the rights of workers, although how that fitted with George Eames senior's Catholic heritage I could never fathom).

If there were concerns about George senior's political leanings there seemed few about his reputation as a footballer; according to some, he was one of the best backmen for the Albury Football Club in the Ovens and Murray League. It was a passion inherited by most of his sons. After running for Richmond with his brother Tom, Jack came back to captain and coach Wodonga. My father played under Jack for Wodonga but on the field there was no chance of ever confusing the two of them. Short and with bandy legs inherited from his mother, my father's on-field performance as a back pocket player was in striking contrast to the taller Jack's seemingly effortless, flowing style, a contrast the *Border Morning Mail*'s football writer once felt compelled to recognise after the match, by describing Jack's performance as 'elegant and controlled' and my father's as 'workmanlike, but not pretty'.

I never knew whether my uncle Sid could play football and no one in our house talked much about Frank and Phil, even though Frank became a valuable part of Jack's Wodonga team when my father left to captain South Albury. As for Jeff, I don't think he ever pulled on a football boot, which meant no one talked about him at all. Of all the brothers though, it was mainly Dave and George junior who had the most impact on my father's world, but both for very different reasons.

2

Hanging up his boots

My father's last two years of playing football were not happy ones for any of us. Even after he'd stopped playing for Wodonga and been appointed captain and coach of South Albury, I think he could see the writing on the wall that his football career was coming to an end. Not that all the writing was on the wall; as the years of ritual neared their end, most of it seemed to be on his arms and legs.

After a hard week of work as a spare parts man at Preston Motors (in the days before he unexpectedly turned his hand to undertaking), my father looked forward to weekends. But I could see why my mother hated them. Every Saturday before we headed off to the match she would pack Dad's footy shorts, socks, boots and guernsey into his Gladstone bag. It seemed to be the Gladstone bag more than anything which marked you as a footballer in those days, it being right up there with the number on the back of your guernsey and the leather stops on your football boots. Bulbous and brown with a concertina top and sliding locks at each end, it carried everything that was clean to the match and everything that was dirty home again. Occasionally my mother would even put Dad's lunch in it, but what the stench of liniment and sweat would have done to his tomato sandwiches I could only imagine.

Once at the ground he and the bag would disappear into the change shed, that male-only world where they slapped each other on the back, told jokes and laughed noisily as they donned their uniforms and prepared for battle. What came out of the player's gate, at least in my father's case in those last two seasons, would be a completely different person, someone who looked like he'd been let out of the back of an ambulance, half running, half hobbling, with straps around both knees and ankles and another around his left elbow.

His appearance was also not helped by the need to leave his false teeth in the Gladstone bag, which meant that whenever their captain shouted instructions or a change of on-field tactics to the other players it came out more like a slushing, slurring sound rather than something you could easily undertand. Still, the other players in the team must have been able to make out what he was saying because they won the premiership that year. That should have meant Dad left his football career on a high note, but we all knew things were never going to be the same again.

When the next season's Tuesday and Thursday training nights came around he was no longer a participant in the drama and intensity of it all, his own voice now gone from among the urgent shouts and ball calls between dimly lit figures as they disappeared into the darkened end of the field on sprinting and handball drills. For my father, those nights gave way instead to extended after-work sessions at the Terminus Hotel, long silences over the evening meal and a general grumpiness which was relieved only by an early departure to bed.

Saturdays were even worse, with added time at the Terminus after the morning's work, and it seemed not even the closest of matches in the Melbourne league could replace the smell of liniment or the camaraderie of battle which had been the focus of Dad's life for so long.

So when Uncle Dave turned up at our back door one Friday night with two bottles of beer under his arm and said he wanted to talk to Dad about a second football career, umpiring, Dad looked delighted to see him.

Maybe it was because Dave was the eldest of the brothers that my father always looked up to him, getting Dave's opinion on just about everything he thought mattered—which may have been why my mother didn't like Dave very much. Although I think it had more to do with what Dave was now proposing.

While Dave Eames had been a handy footballer in his day, he'd stepped away from playing the game to follow other sporting pursuits—firstly boxing, which he must have been reasonably good at as Dad said he'd once fought a draw with Fred Hannaberry who later became Australian middleweight champion. Lately though, he'd become a leading light in the Albury Umpires Association which, in my mother's case at least, didn't seem to help him much.

I could tell by the look on her face when Dave first mentioned the word 'umpiring' that she wasn't going to be happy with any such development. Apart from believing she'd seen the end of dirty shorts, sweaty jock straps and wet socks, she always carried doubts about Dave's motives, reckoning that when Dave had a suggestion to make to my father it was more to Dave's benefit than to the recipient's.

I could see the problems from her point of view. Added to any shortcomings she might have associated with my uncle Dave, it was always obvious that football was something she didn't like but had married and had to live with. And as for umpiring: well, if you were a member of a football team at least half the spectators could be counted on to be on your side. However, she'd seen enough of Aussie Rules to recognise that *nobody* liked the umpire, who was little more than a target for legally sanctioned abuse.

So while Dad and Uncle Dave talked about the subject over the kitchen table, my mother uncharacteristically made her feelings obvious by crashing dishes in the sink, slamming cupboard doors and occasionally glaring at my father from behind Dave's back as she moved around the room. Not that anyone took any notice, as Dave explained the structure of the umpire's association and kept beefing up the umpire's importance to the game.

'Think of it Mick,' he said. 'You can't have a game of football without an umpire.'

I could see the effect of these words on my father, who was already picturing himself back in the centre of things, replacing the spotlight of South Albury captain and coach with the glow surrounding the man in white, the controller of the game.

'Tidge,' Dave said to Dad, 'you can stay involved in the game and earn a few quid's worth of drinking money.'

There it was, and I could see Mum visibly sag—Dave's use of Dad's intimate family nickname and the lure of an extra beer or two.

Dave left soon after with a self-satisfied look on his face. He didn't even seem to notice the one on my mother's.

Dave's umpiring association covered games within a hundred-mile radius of Albury, so by the time the football season started my father had arranged to borrow an old Chevrolet from Preston Motors. Our Saturday world was from then on marked by long drives to places like Chiltern, Walla, Walwa, Mitta Mitta, Eskdale and Dederang. But it was different now. Instead of the laughter and jokes of a car filled with team players, they were solitary drives with Mum in the passenger seat silently knitting a jumper for my bother Pete.

Gone also were the cheery smiles and welcoming waves on arrival at the ground. They were replaced by furtive sideways glances designed to avoid eye contact, broken only by clipped instructions from an official directing my father to the remotest part of the dressing sheds where he changed on his own, as if any contact with the players would taint the outcome of the clash.

The grounds were all pretty much the same: a grassed area in the middle of the town with little more than a rudimentary wrought-iron dressing shed, four goal posts at each end of the oval, sometimes painted white, sometimes still bearing the original sapling grey and often not even straight. Most times there was a single railing fence, wobbly here and there, marking the demarcation line between players and spectators; sometimes there was nothing at all, often resulting in a chase for the ball near the boundary ending up in a tangle of players' arms and legs among picnic lunches and thermos flasks.

For the first few games Mum would spread out a rug and we'd sit on the edge of the oval, usually well away from the majority of the crowd who mostly gathered in front of the dressing shed or behind the goal posts, where they could try to second-guess the goal umpire's decisions. But the rug lasted only two or three matches until my mother's suspicions about my father's widespread unpopularity were confirmed, and we retreated to the relative anonymity of the front seat of the Chev. And by the time we arrived at Balldale for the last home-and-away game of the season even that had become too much for her.

There are really two different games played in a season of Aussie Rules. The first are the home-and-away games, where each team meets each opposition side on its home ground. And while the points for a win marking your climb up the league ladder are important, there's still an air of friendship and sportsmanship about it, as if the game's the thing, and not necessarily the win. Even the odd contested umpire's decision isn't seen as the end of the world.

All that changes when the finals arrive. That's when, no matter whether you're a player or a club supporter, your very reason for being is now under threat. Lose this stoush and you might not exist for the rest of the season. Farmhand mates who share a tractor seat during the week and a beer in town after work will knock each other's block off to get hold of the ball if they play for opposing teams. Supporters will lose all tolerance for an umpire's decision. A decision is either their team's way or it's wrong. And here was my own father, right in the middle of it, at Balldale.

A win over the opposing team on this day would see Balldale go into the finals. By the time Dad blew the whistle to bounce the ball for the start of the match there were so many people that we were having trouble seeing past the crowd standing between the Chev and the boundary fence. Not that it worried Mum much, as she wasn't all that keen on watching anyway.

She knitted quietly through the first half and when Dad came over to the car to get a drink at half-time none of the spectators took any notice of him. But by the time the bell sounded for the start of the final quarter you could tell something had changed. Balldale were trailing and according to the majority of bobbing heads across the bonnet of the Chev it was largely my father's fault, because they were shouting at him from all directions.

Most of the noise was coming from a short, pug-faced man in front of us who was becoming more and more agitated and going through a strange ritual. He would slowly squat down then leap to his feet with a shout every time Dad made a decision in favour of the other team, ripping off his hat and waving it up and down violently as if he was trying to wave away blowflies. He would then slam his hat down on his knee. Once, the man next to him had to grab him by the arm to stop him running onto the ground.

It wasn't easy to see what was going on out in the centre, just occasional flashes of white as my father appeared and disappeared with the flow of the game through spaces between the bobbing heads in front of the Chev's radiator.

Mum, knitting now as if she had to finish Pete's jumper by the end of the game, only spoke once when we caught a glimpse of white.

'I wish he could stay on the other side of the ground,' she said. But I'm sure she knew things would be as bad over there.

Just when we thought it would never end the final whistle blew. For a few seconds there was a stunned silence from the crowd in front, then, as one, they began shouting and waving their arms at each other and in the direction of the centre of the ground. I could see Mum look in horror as a big man who had been watching the match on his own off to our right started to run out onto the ground towards where my father was standing with a dazed look on his face. Someone had given him back the football and he was holding it in his hands as if he didn't know what to do with it, while all around him the winning team's players were jumping up and down, intermingled with Balldale players who were walking off the ground with heads downcast.

At first I thought the big man might have been a friend of pug face. But after he dodged in and out of the players to reach my father he put his arm around Dad as if he was an old friend and led him off the field, disappearing through all the people who had surged over to line up at the gap in the wooden boundary fence near the dressing shed. A few minutes passed before they both suddenly appeared again at the door of the car where the man introduced himself to Mum as the local policeman. He handed Dad his Gladstone bag and suggested we drive straight home. I doubt Dad had any intention of doing anything else, really, as he was still in his white shirt, white shorts and football boots and not even my father would have enjoyed a drink at the Balldale hotel that day.

Not one word passed across the front seat on the drive home that afternoon and it was probably fortunate that Dad didn't draw any further umpiring assignments for the remaining finals matches that year.

He told Dave a few days later he was withdrawing from the umpire's panel next season. As it turned out, that Saturday at Balldale was to be the last occasion Dad would pull on his footy boots as an umpire, which was just as well as I think my mother would have ridden her bike up to Uncle Dave Eames' place in East Albury and thrown them at him.

3

Dad, Uncle George and Flora's cubbyhole

We didn't see much of Uncle Dave after my father's umpiring career came to an end. But it didn't take long for my mother to start worrying about the substitutes, which in my father's case were the Terminus Hotel and my uncle George.

The Terminus had, of course, always been there but it now became what appeared to be an extension of my father's job at Preston Motors, the General Motors dealer just up the road from our house in Townsend Street.

While my mother may have occasionally referred to it as his second home it wasn't much of a place by those standards, just an undistinguished two-storey brick building at the far end of Albury's main street, across the road from the main Sydney to Melbourne railway line. Nobody ever called it the Terminus, though—everyone knew it as McLennan's, after the licensee Flora McLennan, a big, gruff woman who always wore black and appeared to intimidate her clientele, not only because of her size but because she had the power to turn off the after-hours tap.

Six o'clock closing meant that every hotel in Albury had an after-hours beer tap. But my mother was convinced that the after-hours tap at McLennan's put in more hours than the rest of them combined, which meant that Flora McLennan, Bill Lester and my uncle George, among others in the know, saw more of my father than she did.

The moment Preston Motors' doors shut at five o'clock each day my father's first stop would be McLennan's. If McLennan's hadn't been forced to shut at 6 p.m. we probably wouldn't have seen my father until ten o'clock at night. My father would arrive home around 6.30, have dinner and then leave again in time to take part in what he called his evening 'session'. This took place around what was known as the cubbyhole, a small white sliding door around eighteen inches square, at about waist height in the back wall of the hotel. It opened into what could be termed a sort of beer garden.

Only Flora's better customers ever made it to the cubbyhole and even any outsider introduced by a regular felt he was under suspicion because of the ever-present fear of the New South Wales Police Flying Squad. Everyone hated the Flying Squad. They roamed the state like uniformed vigilantes, carrying out lightning raids to catch hotels trading after hours and therefore putting the hotel's liquor licence at risk. I once heard Dad tell my mother with some pride that Flora hardly had to worry because she had a good friend at the Albury police station who would give her a ring if he heard the Flying Squad were in the vicinity.

Dad said the main reason the cubbyhole was out the back was so that, if necessary, it would take Flora only a second or two to turn off the tap, collect the glasses and slam shut the cubbyhole door from the inside. The Flying Squad would be none the wiser. Since my father and the rest of the drinkers were outside the main building anyway, all they had to do was make a run for it through the beer garden, across the gravel car park and over the paling fence into the paddock behind, there lying low until the police left and in the hope that Flora would re-open the cubbyhole.

It was my uncle George who told Mum that my father was largely responsible for the cubbyhole being there in the first place. Before then, everyone used to drink in the front bar with the lights out after closing time, until one night when the tip-off came very late. Flora didn't realise that the Flying Squad were there until they appeared in the car park. She whispered for everyone to get out quietly through the lounge next door but my father decided otherwise, figuring his best chance was to leap behind the bar, crouch down and make a run for the hotel's side exit door.

While the others scurried out towards the lounge, my father, showing a commendable degree of athleticism, launched himself across the bar, only to have one foot hit the stack of glasses hanging down from the rack above. There was a shattering noise as glasses hit the bar and the hotel floor but my father wasn't hanging around to clean up the mess. When the police came through the door a few seconds later the shattered glass apparently made it quite difficult for Flora McLennan to convince them there had been nobody in the bar just before they arrived. Uncle George said Flora was so furious with my father she insisted he pay for the broken glasses or be banned from membership of the after-hours drinking group, something which Uncle George said had been an easy decision for my father to make.

It was hard not to like my uncle George, even though he was one of the main reasons we didn't see much of my father beyond meal times. They were ill-matched in many ways, George's complete lack of interest in football contrasting with all of my father's other friends. Part of their bond had something to do with George's sense of humour and carefree approach to life, which included a talent for practical jokes that my father always aspired to but could never quite match.

Taller than most of his siblings in a gangly, awkward way, George's shock of blond hair sat above a round, friendly face that always appeared on the edge of a smile. This was probably fortunate as there never seemed to be anything serious about my uncle George, just an endless stream of comments which took hold of the funny side of everything, no matter how serious the subject. Even his laugh, which often arrived mid-sentence, had its own humorous trigger, starting as a low, barely audible gurgle before developing into a series of gasping, choking sounds from somewhere deep down in his throat as his face gradually turned crimson. When it finally exploded into the open you got a three-way choice of either laughing at the joke itself, at the weird guttural noises coming from his throat, or you could just be swept up in his own infectious enthusiasm for the humour of the story he was telling. But from my father's viewpoint, his relationship with George had more to do with George's rare talents at the controls of anything with four wheels and an engine than with his sense of humour.

George had become something of a legend in his own driving lifetime at the wheel of a timber jinker in the mountain country of north-east Victoria. Up there they talked about George as if he was some wheelborne equivalent of The Man from Snowy River, his exploits behind the wheel the high point of many a conversation among the timber cutters gathered across the pub bars at places like Mitta Mitta, Omeo and Eskdale long after George and his mechanical horse had parted.

George drove for Dunstans, owners of the big mill at Sunnyside, an old gold mining settlement above Glen Wills where the valleys were short on sunlight even at the height of summer and snow covered the surrounding peaks in winter. Apparently the legend had been borne in the late thirties and early forties when George's long, cumbersome, log-bearing Ford ruled a twisting, corrugated gravel road between the mill, Glen Wills and Mitta Mitta barely wide enough for a large car let alone a timber jinker. It was a road that had merely been hacked around the edge of the mountain, on one side the dark foliage of tree and scrub rising towards the mountain top and on the other a drop of hundreds of feet into the river gorge below.

The big blue Ford was an ugly, long-nosed beast with no trailer brakes. All George had between himself and a spectacular plummet over the edge were the Ford's rudimentary prime mover brakes and the timely use of the gears to hold back the gravitational push of eight tons of logs straddling the bogies behind the truck's cabin.

It was little wonder that my father, who regarded his own driving as an art form, was in awe of George.

'It's as if George and the engine are talking to each other all the time,' he would say by way of explaining how George could go up and down through the gears without using the clutch. George did this as if it was the natural thing to do, something which required exquisite timing and use of just the right amount of revs via the accelerator to mesh with the Ford's primitive crash-type gearbox.

Once my father even admitted he'd made some money out of George's talent. There was reverence in the way he recounted how they'd been drinking in the Mitta Mitta pub one day and a couple of strangers in the bar refused to believe my father's story of how George could change from first to reverse in the big Ford without using the clutch. 'C'mon, George. Show 'em how it's done,' suggested my father.

'I dunno Mick, it's hardly worth the effort,' replied George. He was either playing hard to get or was too interested in finishing the beer on the bar in front of him.

'You'll have to, mate,' said my father, nodding towards the locals. 'Some of us have already put a few quid on you.'

Since any hint of extra drinking money was sufficient to get George to do almost anything, bets were confirmed and my father, George and the rest of the patrons in the bar were soon standing alongside the big Ford watching George climb into the cabin to start the engine. Then, without any fanfare the Ford moved forward a few feet, reverse was selected and the deed was done, without the slightest hint of a clashing of the gears. I could just imagine my father bursting with pride at his brother's prowess as he collected the winnings.

As for George himself. He didn't seem to take his driving talents seriously at all, the tall mountains and narrow roads simply serving as a canvas for his communion with the big Ford, interspersed with a few light-hearted distractions along the way—even if they were sometimes at the expense of his own brothers.

Part of the George Eames legend had grown around a tall, ramrod-straight ironbark tree which reared up from the the edge of a hairpin bend halfway down the mountain between Glen Wills and Mitta Mitta. All the locals knew it well and years after George and the Ford had disappeared from the road would still point it out to visitors as George Eames' tree, the only substantial piece of timber at that point of the road which stood between the edge of the gravel and a four-hundred feet drop into the river below.

The hairpin was so sharp that even a normal tray-body truck had to swing dangerously close to the precipice to negotiate the corner. When it came to a long, log-laden timber jinker it required a whole sequence of turns, interspersed with backward and forward manoeuvres, to get the truck safely around the bend.

George, however, had devised a technique whereby as he approached the notorious lefthander he would aim the truck at the outer edge of the road then swing the steering wheel at the last minute so that the logs on the back of his semi would protrude out over the drop and begin to rub against the ironbark. Then, by reversing and going forward several times George would gradually ease the vehicle around the bend, all the while using the tree rubbing along the logs to stop the truck slipping over the edge.

My father first heard the story from uncle Jack, who said it allowed George to navigate the hairpin in half the time of the other drivers. Uncle Jack could tell the story because he and Uncle Jeff had experienced the process first-hand, although I could understand why we never heard the story from Uncle Jeff.

They'd set out from Glen Wills fully loaded one afternoon after Jack, a few years older than Jeff, had used his seniority to ride in the comfort of the cabin with George. This meant that Jeff was relegated to sitting atop the front of the logs, just behind the cab. Not that Jeff would have cared too much, really, as despite the chill in the air his elevated position gave him a bird's-eye view of proceedings as they motored down the mountain. That was, of course, until they reached the hairpin. George immediately went into his unique turning routine with the big ironbark and Jeff suddenly found himself staring straight down at the river four hundred feet below, as the logs brushed backwards and forwards against the tree. Within seconds he was scrambling along the top of the logs towards the back of the truck and leaping down onto the roadway.

Mesmerised by George's technique, and from the relative safety of the cabin, the first Jack saw of Jeff's plight was a glimpse of his younger brother, visibly shaken, standing in the middle of the gravel road behind the truck. Then he saw the sudden look of panic on Jeff's face as George, the tree-rubbing manoeuvre successfully completed, drove off down the mountain. They'd travelled several hundred yards before Jack thought he'd better alert George that their younger brother was running behind the truck frantically waving his arms for them to stop. George brought the truck to a gradual stop just long enough for Jeff to clamber back up behind the cab. It wasn't until they set off again that George at last broke the silence, turning to Jack with a wry grin on his face and saying, 'I wondered how he would react.'

After that, accompanying George from Glen Wills to Mitta Mitta became something of a badge of honour for the Eames boys. Even if they couldn't brag about George's exploits on the football field, at least his prowess behind the wheel was a worthy substitute. But if anyone ever criticised George for lacking any sporting ability, my father was always quick to defend him. After all, he was there the day George fought the Alabama Kid.

4

Uncle George and the Alabama Kid

You have to live in the country to appreciate what a country show means. I know the pictures always show the prime cattle on parade or Mrs Mullarvey with her prize-winning sponge, or a pumpkin half the size of a box trailer. But they never seem to capture the atmosphere of Sideshow Alley, where the spruiker from the Fat Lady's tent is almost drowned out by the rasping throttles from the motorcycle Wall of Death.

Sideshow Alley on the Saturday of the Albury Show was like a magnet to my father and his two brothers Jack and Dave. They always went together because, having done a bit of boxing and refereed some fights at the Albury Palais on Saturday nights, Uncle Dave knew a few people associated with Harry Johns' Boxing Troupe—and I think Jack and my father liked to bask in some of the glory that attracted.

They'd arranged to meet at Harry's tent as soon as my mother headed off to watch the trots. By the time Dad and Jack found Dave, the crowd was overflowing into the narrow walkway which separated Harry's tent from the other shows in the Alley. Harry Johns, megaphone in hand, was already in full flight on the platform a few feet above their heads, describing the attributes of his brood, occasionally turning aside to point towards one of the larger-than-life canvas images of fighters who peered down from the stage backdrop at the mere mortals in the Alley below, their fearsome facial expressions highlighted by fiery eyes that dared anyone to challenge them.

Today's centre of attraction was this year's champion, a big-boned black fighter from the American south who went under the title of the Alabama Kid.

Just as all eyes settled on the Kid's canvas image on the stage backdrop, Harry waved towards the tent flap. Out onto the stage burst the real thing, already stripped down to his boxing shorts and boots, his gloved hands flailing the air as he pranced up and down the platform behind Harry. Flexing his dark brown biceps and glaring down at the crowd, he exhorted the spectators, attempting to entice a suitable challenger.

'This is all bullshit,' Dave said to Dad. 'Any search for local talent is unsuccessful most of the time. Nah, what usually happens is one of the troupe's own fighters, posing as a local, accepts the challenge. And that's easy in a big place like Albury, where you've got out-of-towners mixed with Albury locals in the crowd.'

Dave had hardly finished explaining all this when there was a shout from the far side of the throng. The Eames boys snapped their heads in that direction as the crowd began to part, and the tall, slightly dishevelled figure of George Eames lurched towards the marquee.

'Jesus, what's that silly bugger up to?' Dave gasped as he watched his younger brother start to climb the steps at one end of the stage, almost tripping on the last one but recovering in time. There was a brief cheer from the crowd as George, white shirt half out and one shoelace undone, threw a series of short jabs into thin air and in the general direction of the Alabama Kid at the far end of the stage.

Dave wasn't one of those cheering though, the look of consternation on his face evidence that he had no illusions about George's fighting ability. But he could see it was too late to stop it now as George, with one arm draped affectionately around Harry Johns' shoulder, slurred something into the megaphone about knocking the Kid 'into the middle of next week', punching the air again as the crowd gave another cheer.

Uncle Dave was already moving. 'C'mon,' he said to Dad. 'I'm going in as his second. At least we can keep an eye on him.' He led off towards the entrance to the tent.

It was dark inside but once their eyes became accustomed to the half light my father and Jack and Dave could just make out a few tiers of wooden seats and some standing room on the grass around a ring which had been created in the centre—or what would be more accurately described as some sawdust-covered canvas inside a roped-off square. They lost Uncle Dave for a few seconds in the pushing and shoving as everyone scrambled for the best vantage points. By the time he'd reached ringside Dave was already talking earnestly to George, who was now stripped, gloved and bouncing around just inside the ropes. It was obvious George wasn't taking much notice of what Dave had to say, his ruddy face broken by a broad grin which became even broader every time the crowd shouted encouragement.

There must have been a few there from the timber country up Mitta way because my father heard someone yell, 'Give 'im one for Omeo, George,' to which George punched the air in their direction with several exaggerated movements, before Dave managed to coax him back into the corner. Then the bell went and Dave turned to Dad.

'He's pissed,' Dave said. 'I reckon he's been in the bar all morning.' But I think my father had probably already worked that out.

In the first few minutes George, his pale body contrasting sharply with the dark features of the Alabama Kid, seemed to be all over the ring—stepping back and forth in his bare feet, jabbing his gloves towards the Kid's nose as if to tease him, then dancing back out of reach as the Kid countered with a left or a right, which George initially avoided by staying just out of reach. George even landed a few punches. But as the round continued the Kid kept coming at him, moving forward all the time, slowly and deliberately, like a big cat stalking its prey. Soon the Kid began to score a few hits of his own, each one slowing George down a little, until, by the time the bell sounded for the end of round one, even his originally light-footed moves in backing away from the Kid had become an occasional backward stumble.

As George flopped onto the corner stool, breathing heavily, Dave squeezed through the ropes, shouted for Dad to pass some water from the bucket beside the ring and started to douse his brother's battered face and upper body with water. While Dave began fanning him with the towel George was rolling his head from side to side as if trying to exercise his neck muscles. My father couldn't help but notice a dazed look on George's face and wondered at first if George could hear what was Dave was saying as he offered him some encouragement: 'You're going all right, mate. He's hardly laid a glove on you.'

To which George, rivulets of blood and sweat mixing with the water trickling down his face, replied through bleeding lips, 'Christ Dave, if that's the case you'd better keep an eye on the referee. Some bastard he is!'

It didn't last much longer. The ref George had been concerned about stopped the fight midway through the third round when the Kid landed a few quick blows to the head and solar plexus, and Dave threw his bunched-up white towel over the ropes—it landed on the floor of the ring about the same time George did.

George's lips were still swollen and you could see a bruise around one eye when he called in at our place a few nights later. Dad insisted he tell Mum the story about how it all happened. George just smiled and said he couldn't remember much.

'I hit him in the face with my fist,' he said, 'and the next thing I'm being accused of looking up some woman's dress at the back of the crowd.'

Even Mum could see the funny side of that. Though for some time now you could tell she was finding it hard to see the funny side of much else—football had receded further and further into my father's past and he was finding it more difficult to replace it with anything, least of all work. At times like this he took it out on my mother as if it was somehow her fault. They'd begun to argue more frequently, particularly when my father would complain about Preston Motors and his lack of promotion, which he said was all to do with religion.

'The place is run by Freemasons,' he said, 'and there's no way a Catholic like me is going to get anywhere there.' This would be the signal for my mother to counter with the accusation that it might have something to do with him spending too much time at the Terminus Hotel. Later, even after they had gone to bed, I could still hear them arguing. Whether the problem was with the Freemasons or the Terminus was never resolved, because it was about that time the tall man from Holbrook turned up with a job offer which was to eventually set my father on his career as a country undertaker.

And the fact that the man from Holbrook was a good Catholic probably helped, too.

5

Holbrook here we come

Like my uncle Dave and his Umpires Association, Ignatius Patrick Kane—Nace—arrived at our house one night with two bottles of beer under his arm, although the reception he got from my mother contrasted markedly with the one she'd given Uncle Dave.

This time there was no slamming of cupboard doors or clashing of dishes in the sink. She even took part in the conversation around the kitchen table, which was peppered with mentions of new challenges and a prosperous country town up the Hume Highway and a rent-free house next to Kane's Motors. From her point of view though, the whole discussion probably had more to do with restarting my father's spare parts career as far away as possible from Uncle George and Flora McLennan's hotel and the Freemasons at Preston Motors.

Even though, as he left, Mr Kane said he'd give them a few days to think it over, the very next night I heard my father say, 'He's offered us a car, Edna. It's a 1929 Chev ute. I saw it today. He's been trying to sell it in Albury but he'll give it to us if I take the job.'

Within a week the Chev was loaded with our most important possessions and we were on our way to a town forty miles north of Albury on the Hume Highway—to a 'whole new future', as my father had started to call it.

It was hard to think of Holbrook without thinking of two things, really; the first of which was the Hume Highway which, in an arrow-straight stretch of a mile or so, split the town exactly in half. The second was the richness of the Riverina countryside, which my father said was one of the best examples of that part of Mr Menzies' Australia that rode on the sheep's back. Nurtured by grazing families who had been on the land for generations, their vast holdings were broken only by soldier settlers who had been granted chunks of the bigger properties as a reward for their war service. Not that you could ever tell them apart when they came into town, as they all wore the same light-coloured trousers, long-sleeved shirts, soil-scuffed riding boots and broad-brimmed hats.

As for the town itself, there were three hotels, all named geographically, as country folk tend to do. They might have been originally christened with high-sounding names such as the Holbrook, the Riverina and the Criterion, but to the locals they were simply the Top, Middle or the Bottom Pub. Which one you regularly drank at depended on how friendly you were with the particular publican, which we somehow guessed would never be a problem for my father.

There was everything else that mattered in a country town: an RSL Club, a golf club with sand greens, a district hospital, and three general stores. One of these, Mackie's, didn't rate a cash register but relied on you getting your change via a pneumatic pressure system. It propelled your money, in a small wooden cup, through the air along a wire trace above the display shelves to the accounts desk on the mezzanine floor. The cup was eventually returned with your change and the receipt protruding from the side of the cup's screw top.

Mackie's red-brick façade, along with the nearby police station and the Bottom Pub just across the road, balanced Holbrook's southern end, separated from the rest of the town by the highway bridge over the Ten Mile Creek. After that, the imposing red brick of the shire hall-cum-picture theatre took over and dominated the central part of the town. From there, the main highway surged north past little clusters of shops, two churches and the post office until finally reaching the Top Pub which anchored the town's northern edge. The road then disappeared north towards Sydney, several hundred miles and another world away.

Like the highway that divided it, the name Holbrook itself had something of a split personality when you thought about it. They'd originally named it Germanton, after some settlers of German descent. But the call to patriotism which came with World War I saw the name quickly fall out of favour as Australian lads began dying on the fields of Europe. Fortunately, a Royal Navy Commander called Norman Holbrook helped solve the problem when he won the Victoria Cross for sinking a Turkish battleship in the Dardanelles, and the local councillors took the opportunity to choose a name more appropriate to the times.

While the squatocracy ruled the countryside, it would soon become apparent that my father's new boss, Nace Kane, straddled the town's business community like a colossus, his Kane's Motors strategically placed on the highway opposite the shire hall. Behind its two Shell petrol bowsers on the road verge was my father's spare parts section and a small, glassed-in office separating the town's only car showroom from a workshop which stretched for a half a block in an easterly direction up the Jingellic Road.

Everything about Nace Kane was big. Over six feet tall, he cut an imposing figure, his hair combed back severely above narrow features which tapered down to a small chin. When he spoke it was in the cultured tones of a man who had come from the best of schools, something which my father soon discovered enabled his boss to mix easily in the rarified atmosphere of the Melbourne establishment, where he did most of his business when taking delivery of a sparkling new Chevrolet or Oldsmobile for one of Holbrook's landed gentry.

But as my father would also discover, this was just one example of Kane's natural Irish ability to carry off different characters to suit the circumstances. On their first visit to Melbourne together, to attend the launch party for a new General Motors model at Fishermen's Bend, my father heard the wife of one of the senior General Motors executives, doubtless impressed by the way Kane spoke, ask his boss where he'd been educated.

'Colourville High,' came the reply, which seemed to adequately satisfy the questioner.

Later, in the car on the way home, my father asked Kane where Colourville High was. He expected to hear about some suitably impressive college in either Sydney or Melbourne, only to be told through a cheeky grin that Colourville High was a one-room, one-teacher primary school near Brocklesby, about fifty miles south-west of Holbrook as the crow flies.

'Where did the "High" come from, then?' asked my father.

'It was built on a small sandhill.'

Legend had it that Nace's Irish wiles had also created the circumstances which set him on the path to becoming Holbrook's most successful businessman. Sometime in his youth, and as an acknowledgement of his ability to handle himself with his fists, he'd been chosen by the church elders to accompany one of their monsignors on a visit to Ireland. For some reason known only to them, the elders were a little concerned for the welfare of their colleague due to the uncertain reception he might receive in some areas of the Emerald Isle. So Nace went along as his unofficial bodyguard, a task he must have executed well. So well, in fact, that the church rewarded him on his return with a handsome remuneration. This not only helped establish him as a respected member of the Catholic community but also set him on the path to becoming a respected citizen of Holbrook, which saw him serve terms as shire president, president of the Holbrook Football Club, the RSL club and anything else that mattered in the town.

And my father would soon learn that Nace's Irish heritage also brought with it an edge of impatience and a quickness to anger, which, although short-lived, could be quite devastating while it lasted. Yet few would know that underneath his gruff exterior was a generosity which every Christmas saw him collect a dozen bottles of scotch whisky from one of the hotels and set off around town visiting people both old and young who couldn't afford much cheer in the festive season. He'd hand a bottle of scotch to each, stay for a brief drink and then move on.

In most respects they made an odd couple, Nace Kane with his cultured air masking an Irish temper capable of firing people on the spot then rehiring them later the same day, and my father whose command of the language was expressed in more basic terms, slow to anger but capable of maintaining that anger for a much longer duration. Their only common attributes were their respect for each other's professional ability and their adeptness at seizing an opportunity when it presented itself.

Their first falling out wasn't long in coming and occurred because of my father's decision to buy a partnership in Jim Woolley's taxi.

6

Carrying the live ones first

Stripped back to the basics, an undertaker is in the business of carrying people, so it might appear strange that my father's first venture into the transport industry involved not carrying dead people but live ones. The Eames family had been in Holbrook less than six months when my father's previously unknown commercial streak emerged out of the blue, over a few beers at the RSL club with a local grazier, Jock Hulme, and Jim Woolley.

Jim Woolley, a slightly built, darkly complexioned man who had begun to fill my Uncle George's role as Dad's regular drinking companion, had mentioned he was tired of operating his taxi at night, which must have immediately struck a chord with Mick Eames, known lover of all things driving. Within a trice the deal was done—seventy-five pounds had been borrowed from Jock Hulme, and in a day or so my father had applied for a licence to drive a taxi.

A blue A70 Austin became a permanent feature each evening against the footpath outside our house adjoining Kane's Motors in Holbrook's main street.

Despite my mother's initial reservations, doubtless due to the fact that she had not previously seen this side of my father's character, you couldn't help but fall in love with the A70. Painted deep blue, the side of her elegant sloping bonnet announced her trademark 'Austin of England' in glistening chrome to match the flying 'A' which flared back from the grille towards an interior which bore the residual aroma of old English motoring leather.

Dad matched the A70's colour inside the house with a deep blue cake tin which, he vowed to my sceptical mother, would be the repository of every cent the A70 earned for its new part-time entrepreneur.

That it took only a fortnight to fill the blue tin for the first time should not, perhaps, have come as the surprise it did, as not everyone in a country town at that time owned a car, and those who did only had one per family. So getting home from the RSL club, the Top, Middle or Bottom pubs meant either walking, hitching a ride or calling for the taxi.

With the shearing season upon us the taxi became even more in demand; Holbrook's agricultural dependence meant regular and lucrative journeys to out-of-town properties, as careless shearers and station hands returned from spending their hard-earned wages.

But not everyone was necessarily overjoyed at my father's new venture. I heard a long time later that Nace Kane fired my father twice in the week following the taxi's purchase, but my father kept insisting it was an after-hours only operation until Nace relented. However, according to my father's version his boss had little option but to agree. His main concern had been the intrusion of the taxi into my father's ability to handle after-hours requests for petrol by passing motorists, which my father claimed had never been part of their original deal anyway.

Strangely enough in the end, both sides of the argument would come together with the Kane's Motors robbery.

7

The Kane's Motors robbery

'It's the light from that bloody Shell sign. We've got to do something about it.'

You couldn't mistake my father's tone of voice. It was the same one he used when Vic Gibson's dog got through the back fence and attacked the washing on the clothes line. He was right about the light, although the quizzical look on the face of the owner of the car I was filling up with petrol confirmed that not all three of us knew what he was talking about.

The light attracted them like moths to a flame, but in this case the moths were motor cars and the flame was the yellow perspex Shell emblem on top of the Kane's Motors petrol bowser. It may have been only eighteen inches high and about twelve across, and it hardly emitted more than a pale yellow glow, but to my father it was a flashing neon sign telling every motorist between Sydney and Melbourne that petrol was available, despite the hour. And if there was anything my father disliked doing more than serving petrol after hours I never found it.

The trouble was, Kane's Motors was pretty well at the halfway mark on the Hume Highway between Sydney and Melbourne and, aside from the bigger towns like Albury, there were few garages which operated beyond nine to five. Under these circumstances, if a wise motorist saw a garage serving petrol he dived in, particularly on Sundays and public holidays.

Of course, the fact that they were motorists from the city meant they weren't going to get much credit from my father for anything they had to do with motor cars. According to him, there was a vast chasm between city and country drivers. He'd long been convinced the only place to learn was on country roads, not in some place where traffic lights used your brains for you and convenience never taught you how to calculate your fuel requirements outside the city limits.

Occasionally, when he was in the mood, he'd play his own little game to confirm his opinion, particularly when an after-hours motorist made the fatal mistake of asking him to check the oil. In my father's motoring world, checking the oil was like driving on the left-hand side of the road—it was something you naturally did yourself no matter what your status in life.

'Why don't you check it,' he'd suggest, 'and let me know how much you need.' 'I'll be right back,' he'd say over his shoulder as he disappeared through the front door of the garage, ostensibly to carry out some suddenly remembered chore. He'd be back in a minute or so, leaving it just long enough to see a frustrated motorist peering into the black depths under the bonnet looking for whatever it was that was supposed to tell him how much oil he had. Doubtless feeling pangs of inadequacy, he'd step politely aside as my father would reach down and, with an exaggerated flourish, remove the dipstick and announce the results in a voice that made it clear that the lesson was now over.

Not that this Sunday evening's errant motorist had been subjected to such treatment—the glow of the Shell sign took most of the blame. Although according to my father, it wasn't just the Shell sign's fault. Nace Kane had to take some of the blame for failing to make it clear that the rental advantages which came with living in the house adjoining the garage also came with an after-hours downside.

The problem really came down to the fact that Holbrook was the first sizeable town you came across after leaving Albury to the south and Gundagai to the north. If you failed to remedy a low petrol gauge at either Gundagai or Albury you could be in trouble. Sure, there were petrol pumps in between—at Woomargama nine miles south and one at Tarcutta to the north—but they were at the sort of settlements that resembled ghost towns on a Sunday. Anyway, in Woomargama's case you were already well through the town by the time you realised there was a town there.

Holbrook, on the other hand, had the misfortune of spreading for over a mile along either side of a dead-straight section of the Hume Highway which, in my father's mind at least, meant that any motorist approaching the town at night could see the damn Shell sign from hundreds of yards away. Certainly, there were other garages in Holbrook, but my father was convinced their owners had taken a decision to live in a back street primarily so they could let the load fall on him.

So Sundays and long weekends, instead of simply providing the opportunity to spend more time at the Top Pub or the RSL club, always seemed to bring out the worst in my father, largely precipitated by a knock on the door from a motorist looking for petrol. Although always a model of politeness when handling his spare parts customers during the week, these city folks were a lesser breed and had to be treated accordingly, if they had to be treated at all.

You could see Dad's point of view. It was not so much the single request for petrol but the multiplying effect it had when you opened the pump and began to serve. The moment any passing motorist saw this happening, they would immediately turn in and line up. Before long you had a queue of cars, stretching back up the street past Vic Gibson's place, which was in danger of attracting more all the time.

He'd employed every possible ruse to beat it of course, beginning with asking my mother to answer the door and say he wasn't home. Mum hated telling fibs and for that reason she wasn't very good at it, so if she wouldn't cooperate he'd insist on telling everyone to be quiet until the knocking on the door stopped. Both rarely worked, all too often because the lights in the house were on and conversations in progress when the knocking first started. Sometimes, even after being told Dad wasn't home, the really desperate motorist would simply sit in the car and wait him out, a situation which occasionally forced the Eames family to maintain a fairly restricted lifestyle for an hour or two.

But it was the threat of a queue of cars that was the main challenge to be met, and it was here that my father had made a detailed study of the problem in order to solve it. To operate the petrol bowsers of those days, several actions had to take place. First the front door of the garage had to be opened and the bowser switched on from a panel on the wall just inside the showroom. This would be achieved after a quick look up and down the main street to select a time when there was no traffic approaching. If it was during daylight hours, and since the idea was to have it appear as if nothing was happening, I would be told to stand quietly by the bowser while my father gently opened the door and threw the switch on the wall.

Priming the pump meant you had to twist a star-shaped notch on the side of the bowser, which returned the gallon and cash readouts on the pump to zero. Since the star notch had a ratchet mechanism my father had his own technique, turning it ever so slowly as if each click of the ratchet could be heard for miles around. To further reduce exposure, whoever was serving the petrol would stand between the two bowsers out of line of sight with the road.

Procedures became even more refined if it was night-time, particularly after the mechanics had removed the bulb from the Shell emblem at my father's request, and you soon learned to reach the wall panel without turning on the showroom lights.

But no matter what you did, or for that matter whether it was day or night, the critical period was while you were out there, dangerously exposed, the petrol pump's nozzle in hand, serving a car parked conspicuously alongside the bowser. There was no escape then and the arrival of each additional car meant a further rise in my father's cranky meter. Soon his patience would run out and he would announce that he was turning off the pump. This would usually occur when the driver of the car next in line asked him to 'Fill 'er up', only to have the tank take a mere two or three gallons.

I swear you could see the words 'opportunistic bastard' written all over my father's face but it mostly came out something like, 'That's it. You don't need bloody petrol. You've buggered my Sunday enough,' as he jammed the nozzle back into the bowser slot and slammed the front door, shutting out the shouts of abuse from the remainder of the line.

Afterwards, back inside the house there would be the usual recriminations.

'Bloody Nace never told me this was part of the job when I signed on,' he'd say, although I never heard him tell that to Nace Kane's face. But I think what upset him the most was that there was no chance Nace Kane would be called out to serve petrol; his house was a block away in a back street, just like the others.

Actually, when I thought about it later, neither the Shell sign nor Dad's boss was responsible for what took place on that Monday afternoon of the Queen's Birthday weekend when Mum opened the door to a tall man in an open-necked shirt and grey slacks. He'd tried to fill up at Gundagai, he explained, but found the garages closed and he now doubted whether he had enough petrol to make it the forty miles to Albury.

Dad had been up at the RSL until mid-afternoon and was sleeping it off when Mum woke him. I could hear him grumbling as he came up the passageway, telling Mum so everyone could hear that she should have said he wasn't home. As he stormed out the front door he turned to me as if it was also partly my fault. 'You serve.'

Funnily enough I didn't mind serving petrol. Operating the pump was a grown-up's job and none of the other kids at Holbrook Central School ever had that opportunity. It was also a chance to get a close look at some of the interesting motor cars that passed through. Once, I even served a Bentley and on another occasion an Austin Atlantic, a tourer with a sloping bonnet and the most amazing electric top that came out from behind the back seat at the press of a button on the dashboard and murmured its way to the top of the front windscreen without anyone touching it.

Another day, a man called Frank Kleinig needed petrol and he turned out to be Australia's top motor racing driver. Since Dad loved anyone who could drive a car both fast and well, there was no way he minded us serving Frank Kleinig. They became such good friends that Mr Kleinig would call in every time he went through town to say hullo, whether he needed petrol or not. Once, to my father's delight, Mr Kleinig's car broke down at Holbrook and he hired my father to drive him to Sydney in the A70. Dad returned two days later with one of his most treasured possessions, an autographed photo of him and Frank Kleinig in front of Mr K's Hudson racing car. It may have been the largest single cab fare my father ever collected, but the way he talked about it later I think he'd have driven him there for nothing had Mr K asked.

But there were no Frank Kleinigs, Bentleys or Austin Atlantics this long-weekend Monday. This time it was only the tall man and two other men in a silver Standard Vanguard, which was probably about the most boring car in the world. It had small windows, a cramped interior and a chopped off rear end which gave the impression Mr Standard had lost interest in the task halfway through, ran out of patience and decided to finish it off there and then. What resulted was a front end that looked like a motor car and a back end that had gone missing. Not that my father was taking any notice of it.

'Stand between the pumps and make sure you can't be seen from the road,' he barked. 'I don't want to be here all afternoon,' he continued as he disappeared through the front door of the garage towards the pump switch on the wall.

As soon as I heard the low hum of the pump's motor I began squirting the petrol into the Vanguard, silently wishing the three men would stop walking around the car and move off the roadway, for fear of attracting more customers. Finally, after they'd been talking to each other in little more than a whisper for a minute or so, the two other men looked first briefly at me and then at the gallon counter ticking over in the pump window. They climbed back into the Vanguard, one in the driver's seat and the other in the back, while the tall man, who appeared more friendly, came around to the back of the car.

'Where's your father gone?' he asked, which I thought was a fair question since we hadn't seen Dad since he disappeared through the front door.

'I don't know. I suppose he's gone out into the work-shop for something,' was all I could offer, and he walked off towards the door.

A few minutes later he was back, to be followed shortly after by Dad who arrived just as I finished filling the tank. The tall man gave Dad some pound notes, said he could keep the change for his trouble, climbed into the front passenger's seat and the Vanguard headed off in the direction of Albury.

When Dad started to lock the door I noticed there was just a hint of a smile on his face, probably due to the fact that not only had he received some extra drinking money but if we closed the front door quickly we'd be out of there before any other petrol-starved motorist spotted us. But when I asked him what the tall man had wanted when he went into the garage looking for him, the smile drained from his face. 'What do you mean he "went looking for me?"'

Without waiting for my answer he went back through the door, walking quickly towards the little glass-fronted office in the back left-hand corner of the showroom. Then he was at the door again, running past me and shouting over his shoulder, 'Tell your mother to ring the police and call Nace. They've taken all of the money from the till.' He kept running towards our A70 parked outside the house.

Anything else he said was lost in the engine noise of the A70 as it roared off through the gears towards the south.

By the time the local policeman, Doug Young, had arrived, Nace Kane had been there for ages. Mum had arrived too and didn't seem to know what to do so we went home. She kept making cups of tea and fossicking around in the kitchen, telling me every few minutes or so to go into the garage and ask Nace Kane whether he'd heard anything. He didn't know what to do either and just sat next to the phone talking to Vic Gibson, who'd noticed Doug Young arrive and had come down to see what was happening—although I think it was more than that, because Vic was the local SP bookmaker and needed to know what the police were doing at all times.

After I'd asked Nace the same question two or three times all I received was an impatient shake of the head which doubled as both a 'no' and an imperious dismissal;

he probably figured if he did hear anything he could walk the ten yards to our front door and tell us himself. Dad had been gone for more than two hours when the call finally came. By that stage Mum had been wondering out loud whether he was heading past Albury to Melbourne, Albury being only an hour away from Holbrook.

It wasn't good news. My father was ringing from a farmer's house beside the highway. He'd managed to catch up with the Vanguard just past the Mullengandra pub and the three men must have guessed someone was onto them, as they'd sped up. But the A70 was better than any Standard Vanguard and he'd still managed to keep them in sight while they sped towards the little settlement of Table Top, about nine miles from Albury. It was as they'd approached the long, sweeping left-hand bend where the highway starts to run parallel with the main Sydney to Melbourne railway line, that the dear old A70's sump plug had fallen out, the oil quickly draining onto the road and the engine seizing, leaving both it and my father emitting steam by the roadside and the Vanguard disappearing into the late afternoon sun. Nace tried to cheer him up on the phone by telling him the police were setting up a roadblock further down the highway. In the meantime he'd send the Kane's Motors tow truck to bring Dad and the A70 back.

It was late at night by the time Dad and the A70 made their less-than-triumphant return to Holbrook, limping behind the tow truck. We were all out the front waiting for them. By then Doug Young had told us the police had stopped the car at a roadblock near Shepparton and I thought Dad would be really upset when Nace told him the police had searched the Vanguard from top to bottom but could find so sign of the four hundred pounds missing from the till. 'There's a whole bunch of coppers searching the paddocks near where you blew up at Table Top, where the bludgers reckon they threw out a brown paper bag with the money in it,' Nace told him.

Dad's face seemed to freeze up for a moment and he turned slightly away from my mother.

'Christ, Nace, what are we going to do with this then?' he whispered, pulling a brown coloured object out from inside his shirt.

Nace Kane, too, shot a quick glance in my mother's direction making sure she couldn't hear. He said something about being 'insured', then turning away he slid a brown paper bag into his back pocket and I'm sure I heard him say, 'We'll split it.'

Right up to the time Dad and I had to go to Wagga Wagga General Sessions Court to give evidence against the men, the three of them kept insisting they'd thrown the money into a paddock at the side of the road when they thought the A70 was a police car chasing them. Then a policeman told the magistrate that they'd searched the paddocks for two days but no one ever found out what happened to the money.

I don't think my mother ever found out either. She'd have been horrified.

8

The empire expands

Aside from robberies and missing sump plugs, the taxi brought out something we'd never noticed before in my father. There was a spring in his step which had him walking through the day with a new-found status that part-ownership of the A70 seemed to confer, and gradually the conversations around the kitchen table would turn to how regularly the blue cake tin was being filled and how much more often that would happen if ownership became full-time. He appeared to be drinking less too, which made my mother happy. Although since many of the taxi jobs at night meant pick-up from either the club or one of the three pubs, my mother was never in any doubt that the opportunity was being taken for a quick beer or two with the prospective fare before they set out on the journey.

Neither was my mother too unhappy that the occasional taxi call-out meant frequent interruptions to Dad's card-playing activities with Nace Kane, Jim Woolley and Jock Hulme, which she feared might have been taking some toll on the amount of money that could normally be expected to reach the blue tin under their bed.

Some of my father's confidence seemed to rub off on Mum as well, and along with his talk of leaving Kane's Motors and becoming a full-time taxi owner came an idea of her own—to open a café in a disused shopfront owned by a man called George Fynney, over the road from Kane's Motors.

As it turned out, by the time Jim Woolley had agreed to sell out the taxi licence and my father had broken the news to Nace Kane, my mother had already worked out a lease arrangement with carpenter George Fynney. He would refurbish the interior of the double shopfront with a new Aga stove in the kitchen, a long RAVA bench-type refrigerator to handle ice-cream and milk up the front, wooden shelving behind the counter for the musk sticks and Polly Waffles and five Formica-topped tables for any new customers willing to sample my mother's cooking.

Such a move represented a massive leap of faith for my mother. A naturally shy woman, she was one of six daughters who grew up in South Albury influenced by a mother who insisted they should never force themselves forward.

'Know your place,' she would say over and over again, insisting that a woman's 'place' was always in the background, to be seen but not heard. While several of her sisters broke from the trend and became forceful, independent women in their own right, such was not the case with my mother. She retained a self-effacing shyness which fitted awkwardly with my father's boisterous world of football camaraderie and noisy bar rooms.

But there was no doubt about her confidence in her ability as a cook. She maintained that if you threw into a menu an option of a roast dinner or savoury mince alongside the steak and eggs you'd have no problem attracting customers. So when the opportunity arrived she was determined to grasp it with both hands. Maybe though, her business venture was her way of at last fulfilling a desire to be recognised in her own right, even if it meant taking on a more public persona.

In a way, Holbrook's small town environment made the challenge even more formidable. For while she had no experience running a business, my mother was moving into competition with the only other major eating establishment in the township, Prineas Café, which had long occupied an imposing site only sixty yards away on the corner of the main street and Culcairn Road. But such was her natural, shy charm that she need not have worried. Before the first customer had walked through the wire screen doors of her Australian Café, Jimmy Prineas had already offered her any help she might need to get the business going. In fact, the only awkward moment came when she found herself forced to explain that the name Australian Café wasn't an ethnic slight on Jimmy's Greek origins.

The deal with George Fynney was a simple one: the lease included the shopfront and the kitchen downstairs, along with the three-room living quarters upstairs. This immediately solved the problem of a roof over the Eames family's heads, after having to leave the house adjoining Kane's Motors when Dad had quit. However, George had asked if he could keep using the room behind the café out the back.

That was where he stored the coffins.

Maybe it was while they were talking about the future of the coffins that the idea of Mick Eames, Undertaker, was raised. George Fynney had inherited an undertaking business from his father, but it was no secret around town that George would be happy to see the end of the death business. He'd been captured in Crete at the start of the war and likely he figured he had already seen enough of death and all that went with it.

My father's reasoning for buying the business was probably much simpler; given the sporadic nature of funerals he figured he could easily coordinate the carriage of dead people with the carriage of live ones in the A70. I doubt my mother ever had a say in it at all, which would have suited her as long as he kept the door shut on the back room—the last thing her café patrons wanted to see as they went to the toilet was a bunch of coffins.

9

Get 'em while the tears are falling

It didn't take my father long to work out you didn't get much when you bought a country funeral business.

Basically it amounted to three coffins stored in the room out back, a hearse for carrying the dear departed to their last resting place, a couple of four-by-two planks and two long, grey-coloured, four-inch wide straps to help lower the deceased the final few feet. Still, the theory was that the main 'assets' would come in the future—and not even the future assets themselves knew precisely when that would be.

As for the hearse, well there was a whiff of pride in being the owner of the centrepiece, a 1929 Essex, even though such an American vehicle wasn't all that highly regarded in 1950s Australia.

But you had to admit, as far as country hearses go she was pretty well turned out. Trimmed with chrome side fittings, the black paintwork along her glass-sided rear section touched off with delicately edged borders of gold seemed to set her apart from the rest of the pack. She sat high off the ground on large, wooden-spoked wheels which gave her a superior air enhanced by a flat windscreen which made her appear as if she had a stern look on her face, somehow befitting a hearse. The front doors set her apart too, gently curved across the top, although they came without side windows, her designer apparently assuming it didn't rain on funeral days.

Despite her age and questionable American heritage, once moving she could be a relatively dignified lady, but, as my father's first funeral demonstrated, it was getting her to that point that often presented the main challenge.

A significant part of the problem stemmed from the infrequency of the times she needed to be pressed into service. This forced her to spend most of her time out of funeral hours against the rear wall of Kane's Motors, a dust-covered prop for odd bits of upholstery and discarded mudguard panels.

Initially, despite a wealth of experience gathered over a lifetime dealing with motor cars, it took my father some time to abandon the hope that she might start first go. Once a funeral was in the offing we would start removing the debris around her until he could lift one side of the black bonnet and peer inside as if he needed to check the engine was still there.

'Ok, let's see if she'll start,' he'd offer, ordering me to slip behind the wheel and push down on the metal spike on the floorboard. As the slow groan diminished, signifying defeat once again, there would be a string of curses from under the bonnet followed by, 'That's the trouble with this business. Too much time between funerals.' Which led you to hope no one was passing within earshot along the footpath on the other side of the garage wall, particularly someone with an elderly relative who might be about to 'have a look over the other side' as Nace Kane liked to put it.

It wasn't long before Dad's old Albury funeral director mate Bill Lester arrived for a visit designed to explain the finer points of the undertaking business, along with any short cuts he felt my father could get away with. As the day wore on over a few beers and lunch in the café kitchen, Bill Lester parted with pieces of advice his twenty years' experience had taught him, like the fact that, for some reason, funerals always seemed to occur in threes. No one knew why, he said. It just happened that way. And never, if at all possible, use a cumbersome, expensive vehicle like a hearse for anything except the funeral itself if you could get away with using something else.

Even sample death notices for the *Border Morning Mail* were mapped out, along with the radio announcements for Albury's 2AY, to be finally delivered in a dull monotone along the lines of: 'The cortege will leave the Holbrook Catholic Church at so and so p.m. today for interment in the Holbrook cemetery, etc etc . . .' That assumed the hearse would start, of course.

As for how much to charge, well, that was pretty straightforward, Bill advised:

To burial late Mr__________ .
Silver Mtd Casket
Digging Grave
Conducting Funeral   33 Pounds
Notice to *Border Mail*   10 Shillings

Total   33 Pounds 10 Shillings

Then, just as he was preparing to leave, as if he was saving the worst until last, Bill sounded a warning about outstanding debts.

'Just remember Mick,' he advised my father, 'when they're in the first phase of grief they'll come at you to send the dear departed off with the very best you can do for them, as if no one gives a damn about the expense. 'You'll be surprised how that changes after a few months have gone by and it's time to pay the bill.'

My mother hadn't taken any part in the conversation up to that point but she must have been listening intently and was more than a little concerned about the financial side.

'Well, how do you handle that part?' she asked.

Bill Lester hesitated for a moment and turned as he reached the door. Looking back, not at Mum but at my father and without a trace of emotion in his voice, he answered quietly.

'Mick, always remember that you're the one who's bought the coffin and paid the gravedigger. You've gotta get 'em while the tears are falling.'

10

The gravedigger

You might be excused for thinking that a grave is just a hole in the ground which remains there for a relatively short time before the recipient arrives and it's filled in again. But in fact there's a lot more to it than that, particularly when you're talking about a country town in the 1950s.

For a start, you had to know where to dig and country cemeteries were not renowned for accurately charting the locations of earlier recipients. So an experienced grave-digger was worth his weight in gold, simply because he knew where the bodies were buried, so to speak. And anyway, digging a six-foot deep hole in hard clay or rocky soil wasn't everyone's cup of tea, and the last thing you wanted was to discover evidence of some former citizen halfway through the backbreaking task.

Fortunately, along with George Fynney's Essex and the other bits and pieces, my father had inherited Kelly O'Brien.

There must have been a hundred different stories about where Kelly had come from, all of which were of various colours but had one common thread: that he may have been running from something when he arrived in the district in the 1920s. Most people relied on the version told by Kelly's best mate, Gordon McLaurin, who seemed to have known him longer than anyone else.

The country around Holbrook was a different place in those days and Gordon always claimed Kelly was one of the last of that hardy band of men whose role in opening up the country would go largely unrecognised. Like Kelly, many of them were single men, often with a shady past, who just drifted in on foot and stopped for a few days, a week, a month or two, or never moved on, depending on how they picked up work. Most, like Kelly, camped out on the properties in tents or rough-built huts where they could turn their hand to anything, from clearing scrub and felling trees, to cutting wood, clearing rabbits, shearing sheep or fencing.

They lived a lonely life until, after weeks of no human contact, they would walk out to spend their wages at the nearest of the wine shanties, isolated structures often little more than four wooden walls surrounding a dirt floor and a bar. These had sprung up at intervals along the dusty roads which linked country towns. Solitary men, unused to human contact and with limited social graces, they said little for the first day or so, often worried about being preyed on by some of the less savoury types who frequented such places and who would take the first opportunity to relieve them of their money once they got drunk. To avoid such a fate many of the bushmen would hand over their hard-earned cash to the owner of the establishment for safekeeping, often with the same result, as, once they were drunk, the more unscrupulous among the shanty owners would overcharge them for their liquor and the money would soon run out. None the wiser and after sleeping it off, they would then return to the bush to start the cycle all over again.

Gordon insisted they were proud men, though, who had done as much to open up the country as those who had owned the land itself. He could reel off all the names of those who, when the years caught up with them, had begun to realise they could not continue to live and work that way. They had then simply cashed in their own chips, using the gun, the cut-throat razor or a quick sip of strychnine they used to rid the paddocks of the farmer's pests, until, by the end of World War II, both they and most of the shanties had disappeared from the landscape.

'Kelly would never do that, though,' Gordon told my father when he asked about his gravedigger's background. 'But he's crossed a lot of dry gullies in his time.'

Slight of build but in a tough, wiry way, his leathery complexion honed by years of toil in the bush, Kelly had spent time in reform school as a youngster. He had been on the water bound for the battlefields of France when the war ended and they turned his ship around. He had been carrying his swag down the road from some-where up north when he pitched camp not far from where Gordon lived a few miles out of town, heard a steam engine start up in the shearing shed at Rosslyn station a half a mile or so in from the road and walked over and got a job.

It wasn't long before Kelly and Gordon struck up a friendship and began to team up to earn some money droving cattle across the state. Even then Kelly didn't talk much about his past although, Gordon told Dad, you got to know a bloke pretty well on the lonely nights on the drovers' trails. One thing Dad did find out early on was that his real name wasn't Kelly O'Brien but the less sonorous William Eric Freeburn. The story behind that probably best summed up the sort of character that was our Kelly O'Brien.

Along with an ability to think quickly on his feet and a dry sense of humour, Kelly had a gift for mimicry and could quickly adopt a range of accents which might suit a particular circumstance. Early in the swag-carrying business he'd discovered that an Irish brogue worked wonders when you were looking for a meal or a bed at any of the Catholic presbyteries, a feature of most country towns in southern Queensland and New South Wales at the time. So he took it one step further and abandoned William Eric Freeburn for the much more effective Kelly O'Brien and it worked every time. The name stuck and with the exception of his mate Gordon McLaurin and a few others, most people around Holbrook were none the wiser.

Such a talent for improvisation resided alongside a larri-kin streak which had its own downside, something his mate Gordon had discovered the hard way.

They'd been train-droving a load of cattle to Queensland when the train pulled into Parkes late at night and they faced a two-hour stopover before it resumed its journey. Not wanting to waste the time, they asked the train guard where they might quench their thirst. Pointing to a hotel a few hundred yards away in the dimly lit Parkes Street, the guard said, 'That place never closes. It's a bit rough but you can get a drink.'

The moment he walked through the door Gordon realised the guard hadn't been exaggerating. The place was a bloodhouse—just a board floor, a long beer-splattered bar and a lot of noise, most of it coming from a group of Aboriginal men and women and several large Islanders sitting around a table at one end of the room. But they were thirsty and Gordon told Kelly to order a beer while he went to the toilet.

Gordon had only been gone a minute or so when a burly Islander separated himself from the group and staggered up to Kelly.

'Give us two quid and you can have your pick of the girls,' he said, nodding in the direction of his party who were all now looking in Kelly's direction.

'I don't want any of the girls,' replied Kelly, twisting his head back to look up at the giant confronting him. 'Anyway, we're only here for an hour or so,' he said, at which the big Islander grabbed Kelly by the shirt collar, physically lifting him off the floor.

'Well, give us two quid anyway,' demanded the man, menace in his voice.

It was at that moment that Gordon walked back into the bar, just in time to see Kelly struggling to free himself and pointing at his returning mate.

'Let me go or he'll kill you,' said Kelly. 'He fought Carpontier.'

To Gordon's relief the big fellow dropped Kelly back on his feet, then turned and lurched off to rejoin his group. He had only taken a few steps when, to Gordon's horror, Kelly took several quick paces after him and delivered the hardest kick to someone's arse Gordon had ever seen in his life. Gordon had no intention of waiting to find out what might happen next as the bunch at the table started to rise and kick back chairs. By the time they had gathered themselves he and Kelly were out the door and running as fast as they could towards the railway siding, leaving the pub's very drunk patrons noisily scuffling around behind them in the night.

As the train pulled out of Parkes, Gordon gave Kelly a piece of his mind.

'And anyway,' he asked, 'who the hell's Carpontier?'

'He was a champion French fighter who came out here once,' Kelly said, as if delighted with this opportunity to air his knowledge of the fight game.

'Beat the hell out of everyone, he did,' he said proudly.

Gordon told Dad there might be a bit of a lesson in this for him.

'Take my advice, Mick. Whenever you're having a drink with Kelly, go to the toilet when he goes so you don't have to leave him alone at the bar. Otherwise Christ knows what you might come back to.'

The main problem my father had to get used to in his early days as an undertaker wasn't so much Kelly's surprises at the bar but finding him when there was a funeral in the offing.

Although he lived only a few hundred yards from the Holbrook cemetery on the northern edge of town, Kelly's other work as a fencing contractor took him out into the bush, often for days at a time. So getting hold of him occasionally meant my father skirting the boundary fences in the A70 Austin until he spotted in the distance a solitary figure wielding a crowbar or a shovel along a new fenceline.

Such circumstances often meant Kelly going about his gravedigging assignments in the late evening or at night, so that it would cause the least interruption to his fencing commitments. And while Kelly was never shy of hard work, it turned out he had one thing in common with my father: if there was a short cut or an easier way he had no hesitation in taking it, even if it meant the occasional use of some unconventional methods to get the job done. And since his mate Gordon had a couple of mines on his property, and therefore an excuse for a small store of gelignite, Kelly was not averse to using a half a stick when he struck impenetrable rock or hard clay.

This tendency to take the shortest option also meant that digging a grave didn't necessarily mean you had to dig a perfectly rectangular hole in the ground. Kelly had been at it long enough to realise that a coffin was not rectangular, but broad at the shoulders and tapered at each end. Therefore, if you were smart enough you could 'shape' the grave to the precise dimensions of the casket. After all, any unused inches in a hole in the ground were a waste of time.

That was probably the main reason why the inevitable was bound to happen sooner or later to two people who were inclined towards short cuts.

11

The coffin that wouldn't fit

The new coffins my father ordered were really his way of showing he was a serious businessman now and wanted to change things. So he'd start with the caskets.

You could see his logic, I suppose. You can have all the guest speakers you like at a funeral service, even the highest ranking clergy you can find and even, for that matter, an impressive guard of honour at the graveside, but whether you like to admit it or not, the main focus of attention at the funeral is the coffin. Not that there was that much wrong with the caskets Dad inherited from George Fynney. But by the time the three spares were almost used up he must have felt it was time to put his own stamp on the business.

And true to Bill Lester's tip, they'd happened in threes, and while the first two funerals had gone off without a hitch in the procedural sense, when a workman fell into a well shaft he was digging out on the Culcairn Road, Dad was introduced to a side of the business which nobody talked much about, or envied.

The worker had suffered extensive injuries and retrieving the body from the shaft had taken some time and a lot of manhandling. That night over dinner, my father said very little but I didn't notice anything much wrong until he started to drink his tea. Whether he thought it somehow improved the taste or simply made it cooler, he had a habit of first tipping his tea into the saucer then holding the saucer to his lips and sipping it. But on this occasion his hands were shaking so much that he could hardly hold the saucer steady. After several fruitless attempts he announced he was going to bed and left the table. I wondered whether he got much sleep that night.

The next morning everything seemed normal and he started talking about driving down to Melbourne to talk to the people at H.H. Webb about some new coffins. H.H. Webb obviously impressed my father greatly, showing off a range of coffins of all sizes and wood combinations. But at the end of the day it was the handles which won him over.

While you could never say my father was naturally into detail, he'd already made no secret of the fact that he disliked the handles on the inherited coffins. There were four of them, two on either side—large, silver-coated appendages which were for decorative purposes only. They were attached by four small, ineffective screws and you had to take pains to explain to the casket bearers before every funeral that under no circumstances were they to attempt to lift the coffin by the handles; the slightest weight would have them come away with disastrous results.

Dad figured if he could do away with that possibility it would be just one more detail he wouldn't have to worry about when he went through the coffin preparation procedure. Not that there was much of a procedure involved, and in fact there would have been much less if my father had had his way, inclined as he was towards thinking it was all destined to go to waste below the ground anyway. But even he had to acknowledge there were certain requirements like attaching the handles, along with screwing onto the top of the casket the silver plates with the inscription of the deceased's name and religion.

Dad wasn't in the habit of devoting too much time to the finer points of even that aspect, until the morning Nace Kane called in while he was finishing off attaching the bits and pieces to the coffin of a well-known local follower of the Presbyterian faith.

Nace Kane couldn't believe his eyes.

'Good God Mick, you've got Catholic adornments on it,' exclaimed his old employer, exasperation in his voice. As one of the town's Catholic hierarchy, he obviously knew what he was talking about.

'He won't know,' said Dad, screwdriver still in hand, adopting a defensive tone.

'The ones still alive will, though,' insisted Nace, who remained standing there until he'd convinced Dad it was worth the extra effort to change the adornments.

* *

The day the new caskets finally arrived Dad insisted Mum and I come out the back to see them unloaded from the delivery truck. There were three of them.

'Aren't they bloody beauties?' he said proudly, as he helped the truck driver lift the first one off the truck and carry it into the back room. You could tell from the look on the truck driver's face that he wondered what my father was talking about. A big, heavy-set fellow with short cropped hair and tattoos on his arms, the pained expression on the truck driver's face said quite clearly that his job had been simply to pick up the coffins at the Albury Railway Station when they arrived from Melbourne and deliver them to Holbrook, and such a task didn't require him to imagine for one minute there was anything beautiful about a varnished box used to bury people. Maybe that was why, the instant he placed his end of the last coffin on the floor in the back room he flicked a receipt book from his pocket and pointed to where my father was to sign, then leapt into the truck and drove off in some haste.

As for the coffins themselves—well, you had to admit the new handles my father had chosen gave the coffin a smoother, more stylish look than the originals. Unlike the old fold-down handles, these were firmly fixed, and even though they bulged out slightly from the side of the casket, their curved grips made them appear sleeker and much cleaner. Not only did these handles look better, my father explained to Mum and me, but they were much cheaper than the originals and, at a pinch, could even take a bit of weight, thanks to their sturdier design and larger screws.

The next few weeks appeared to be a proud but frustrating time for my father, who kept taking anyone who called in for a cup of tea or a beer out into the back room to show them his new handles. This was usually accompanied by the comment that he couldn't wait to try them out, even though Mum kept telling him that wasn't the sort of thing you said to people just in case they had an old relative or a close friend who was about to slip away. That sort of thing never worried Dad, though, and you could tell he couldn't wait for the next call to come. When it did, however, it was the last thing he wanted. It was from Woomargama, nine miles south of Holbrook on the Hume Highway. Organising a funeral at an out-of-town venue like Woomargama tended to make things unnecessarily complicated from my father's point of view. If the burial was in Holbrook it was simply a matter of finding out which property Kelly O'Brien was fencing on, driving out to tell him the news and get him started on digging the grave the night before the funeral. This wasn't much of a burden for Kelly, as the proximity of Holbrook cemetery to Kelly's house meant he could usually manage a couple of drinks at the Top Pub after work before he set off to start digging. It was also easy for my father, who had learned that it was a good idea to check on Kelly's progress at least once that night to put his own mind at rest.

Dad had learned this lesson the hard way early on, when he'd decided on the spur of the moment to call at the cemetery on the way home from the Top Pub one evening. Kelly always used an old lantern to help him see what he was doing, but when Dad got out of the car he couldn't see a sign of light anywhere nor could he hear any digging noises. Fearing Kelly hadn't even made a start on the grave, it was with a feeling of increasing concern that he set off towards where the gravesite should have been.

As he got closer he could make out a thin glow falling on a mound of freshly turned earth at ground level. His first thought was that Kelly had suffered a heart attack or some similar misfortune. But he need not have worried. There was Kelly, inside the hole, propped against one end and sound asleep, the still-glowing lantern at one end of the hole and several empty bottles of wine at the other. It took only a second or two of shouting to wake him and get things back on track. Dad always made a habit of calling by after that.

But an out-of-town place like Woomargama meant that the logistics of it all changed.

In the first place Kelly had to be found quickly, to ensure he had the time to head off on the morning of the day of the funeral to dig the grave; given the distances often involved, and with his normal work commitments, there were few opportunities for it to be done the night before. This meant that once Kelly was despatched on the morning of the funeral, the next time my father would see him was when the hearse pulled up at the gate of the Woomargama cemetery with a bevy of mourners in tow.

Now you don't need an elaborate communications plan to run a country undertaking business. Once you've got the basics right, like organising the gravedigger, the timing of the service, the death notice in the local paper and on local radio, and the hearse fuelled and watered, you've pretty well got it covered. Or so you'd think.

Thus, on the face of it anyway, there was little need for much conversation between my father and his gravedigger before Kelly left for Woomargama that morning, although Kelly had made it clear he wasn't too happy about having to sacrifice a full day's fencing for the proceeds of one grave at Woomargama. So he'd left in a bit of a huff, which probably isn't the ideal way for a well-oiled team to work. However, by the time my father turned the hearse off the highway onto the two-wheel track leading to the Woomargama cemetery gate, with me in the front seat as usual, there appeared to have been no damage done, and everything looked to be in order.

It had been raining heavily that morning. We could see a slight mound of freshly turned earth alongside where the grave would be in the top right-hand corner of the cemetery paddock. Kelly, according to my father's instructions, was already standing half out of sight behind a low shrub a few yards away. The positioning of Kelly was one of my father's few concessions to protocol, as he didn't think it was appropriate to have the chap with the shovel appearing too obvious to the grieving relatives.

It had been raining all right, because by the time the hearse was only a few yards into the track the rear wheels began to slip, causing the Essex to lurch sideways. My father fought to keep it from sliding off into the high grass. A quick glance in the rear-vision mirror revealed that most of the mourners had seen what was happening, and were taking the precaution of parking their cars along the edge of the highway and following the hearse on foot.

As the incline steepened, keeping the hearse on the track itself became something of a battle. The wheels intermittently gripped, then slipped, then gripped again until, still twenty yards from the gate, there was a buzz saw-type sound from the rear end as the two back wheels started to bury themselves in the soft mud.

Since the track beyond the gate and through the cemetery was even steeper, there was no way the hearse was going to go any further. With an angry slam of the door, Dad was out and announcing they'd have to carry the coffin the rest of the way. There followed a great deal of slipping and sliding and muffled curses from the volunteers until, their shiny black shoes and suit pants' cuffs covered in mud, they reached the gravesite. They lowered the coffin onto the two four-by-two boards strategically placed across the grave. Dad quickly slipped the two grey lowering straps across the hole as the remainder of the mourners arrived to hear the reverend begin his few words above the coffin.

Just as he got to the part about 'ashes to ashes and dust to dust' it started to rain again, which seemed to make such words sound a bit odd as there wasn't much dust to be seen around Woomargama on this particular day. But the reverend soon finished his burst and the four pallbearers took the strain on the straps as Dad, trying to look dignified in a crouching position, whipped the two four-by-twos away and the coffin began to descend slowly into the hole.

It had only travelled about three feet when the straps suddenly went limp, leaving the four pallbearers looking sheepishly at each other for a second or two, as if wondering why a gravedigger would only dig a hole three or four feet deep. There followed a few moments of frantic pulling and jerking on the straps. Some of the mourners at the back began to nudge forward to get a look at what was happening, but I could tell from the look of panic on my father's face that he'd already worked it out.

The sleek, new, outwardly curved ornamental handles might have come at the right price. But they had made the coffin several inches wider on each side—a fact that my father had either overlooked or at least failed to tell Kelly O'Brien, who had been digging graves to the original specifications for as long as anyone could remember.

In the end, it was the rain that saved any further embarrassment. It was coming down heavily now. After waiting just long enough to see a crestfallen funeral director and a less-than-sociable gravedigger take to the sides of the grave with a shovel and a crowbar to allow the departed to cover the remaining few feet of his journey, one by one and in small groups the members of the funeral party began to see the value in heading down the hill and towards the Woomargama pub. They had decided to start the wake a little earlier than they'd originally planned.

Had any of the mourners waited longer they would have witnessed my father and his gravedigger, oblivious to the pelting rain, engaged in a shouting match over who was to blame for the measurement oversight which had been the first real test of their business relationship. In the end, however, Woomargama seemed to get more of the blame than Kelly O'Brien. Dad didn't even stop for a drink at the Woomargama pub that afternoon and told my mother that he didn't care if he never saw the Woomargama cemetery ever again. Which was probably just as well, as my father appeared to have enough on his plate with the taxi business.

12

The taxi wars

How the different colours of two number plates could develop into a taxi war unlike any Holbrook had ever seen, only those who knew my father could understand.

It may have been that, with the sporadic and unpredictable nature of the funeral business and his growing tendency to spend more and more time at the RSL and the Top Pub, Dad simply had too much time on his hands. This provided him with the opportunity to worry too much about what others were doing and to overlook what he was not doing.

When Jim Woolley handed over the keys to the A70 Austin for the last time there were two other purveyors of hire vehicles in the town. Bob Dexter drove a bull-nosed Nash and unfortunately already had a fractious relationship with my father. This had apparently originated over a dispute they had about football one night at the RSL, although no one who was there could remember any details of the dispute itself. Thereafter they rarely spoke to each other. But that appeared to be only a minor issue when compared to my father's relationship with the other operator, Len Condon.

Slightly built and fair-haired, Len Condon hid a shrewd business brain behind a mechanical engineering talent which had seen him build a fleet of Morris Minor and Morris Oxford hire vehicles. The business had an immaculate grey American D49 Dodge as its flagship and operated from a shopfront further up Holbrook's main street from the Australian Café.

Under other circumstances, Len Condon and my father would have had a lot in common, not least their respect for motor cars, a love of driving and, most of the time at least, an easygoing manner. But right from the start there was no way the two would come to a compromise over the number plates, which all boiled down to what was meant by their different colours.

According to my father's reading of the law, the more expensive and exclusive blue and white number TC3312 on the A70 Austin entitled him to pick up a fare anywhere at any time, particularly from the kerbside while driving around town. Whereas the black and white HV plates on Len Condon's Dodge forbade such plying for trade and his services had to be ordered, or hired, over the phone.

If Len Condon had been stretching the law with his HV plates while Jim Woolley had been operating the taxi it hadn't worried my father's predecessor. But things certainly began to change under the new Eames regime. Any such report of an alleged Len Condon misdemeanour would send my father into a fit of rage, culminating one night when he came home from the RSL club determined to ring the police and dob in Len Condon.

'I've had enough of this. He's still picking up people off the street,' he announced to my mother as he reached for the phone.

Tidying up the kitchen after the last of the evening meal customers had left, it was obvious my mother had no idea what all the fuss was about.

'My goodness, can you be arrested for that?' was her only response. She was doubtless concerned that her husband's action might lead to a jail term for someone.

It wasn't until my father explained the difference to Sergeant Joe Hawkins over the phone that she realised how serious all this was.

'Sergeant?' said Dad, a ring of formality in his voice. Since this was an official complaint to the local constabulary there was no sense using the more familiar 'Sarge'.

'Condon is picking up fares off the street when they wave him down,' he continued. 'He's not licenced for that under his HV plates. If he wants to do that he can buy a blue taxi plate like mine,' he said, throwing the final line out in a superior tone of voice.

While we couldn't hear the other end of the conversation, it was obvious it wasn't going Dad's way.

'Well, what proof do I need?' The tone had now shifted up an octave. 'I've had people tell me he's doing it.'

That didn't seem to work on its own, as after a few minutes he hung up, an exasperated look on his face. 'He's going to send Doug Young up to have a word with Condon. A lot of good that'll do.'

Since my father had extended his conspiracy theory to take in the belief that Senior Constable Doug Young was a friend of Len Condon and his wife, Joe Hawkins' response was never going to satisfy him.

After that, every time my father saw Joe Hawkins he complained about some infringement or other and at one stage Len Condon became so fed up with my father's obsession he moved all his cars off the street and into the lane at the back of his house, just to make them a little less provocative whenever my father drove up the main street. When Joe Hawkins noticed the cars were gone he told Len not to be so stupid and to move them back until he told him otherwise.

Even then I don't think my father realised that nearly everyone except his mates Jim Woolley, Nace Kane and Jock Hulme were on Len Condon's side. Most people thought if Len Condon was picking people up in the street while my father was drinking at the RSL club, then good for him. Neither did he see the signs when the police traffic inspector came out from Albury for his regular visit and gave all Len Condon's cars a clean bill of health yet put the Eames taxi temporarily off the road because of a faulty handbrake adjustment. My mother became so embarrassed by the whole affair that she always apologised to Len Condon when she saw him in the street, because she figured Holbrook was too small a town to worry about such things.

As for the other operator, Bob Dexter, he took no part in the main battle, electing to watch it from the sidelines. But he left no doubt whose side he was on.

'I don't care if Mick Eames is the last undertaker on earth,' he told Nace Kane. 'There's no way he's going to bury me.'

As the weeks went by, still determined, my father changed tactics. He gave Sausage Jamison, the local odd-job man, three bottles of beer to set a trap for Len Condon by waving him down in the street so that he would pick him up. Sausage gratefully took the beer, but every time my father asked him for a report Sausage kept insisting he'd tried to wave Len down but he wouldn't stop for him.

Dad didn't appreciate it when Mum suggested that the first mistake Dad had made was to give Sausage the beers before he'd completed his task.

13

The sausage man

There's a Sausage Jamison in every country town. You know, the bloke who doesn't have a steady job and does odd jobs to keep himself in beer and cigarettes, has no fixed place of abode so sleeps in sheds or wherever he can find a bunk to wear off a perpetual hangover.

Sausage was everywhere yet he was nowhere; he was hard to find when you really needed him, but the rest of the time he was around the Top or Middle pubs chopping wood for the fireplaces, or at the footy ground late on training nights helping to collect the training gear so that the players would buy him drinks back at the Middle Pub. He rarely missed a race meeting and although he never had the money to place a bet he always managed to be somewhere near the bar when the winner of the last race said it was his shout.

It was hard not to like Sausage. Of course, as in the case of Kelly O'Brien, Sausage wasn't his real name. He'd been born Ronald Jamison at Gundagai, further north up the highway but I never heard anyone call him by his first name. He was either Sausage or, for those who had known him the longest, the more intimate Soss.

Of average height and medium to stocky build, Soss walked with something of a loping, forward-leaning stride which gave the impression he was heading somewhere he needed to be when in fact most times there was no-where he needed to be at all. His face, which always wore just the hint of a smile, had a ruddy complexion, the result of both living rough and the ravages of alcohol. This gave him the appearance of a man a lot older than his mid-twenties. The smile helped you accept the odour seeping from the old army great-coat and the dark green gabardine work pants he always wore.

Naturally, there were some who thought Soss a nuis-ance and would even cross the road to avoid him. My father was not one of them; he seemed to have a genuine affection for Sausage, although it wasn't hard to find a practical reason for this as well.

One of the challenges facing an undertaker in a country town is the availability of someone to give you a helping hand with the physical side of the job. While there may be many businesses you can run on your own, undertaking isn't one of them—here, the term 'dead weight' really does have meaning as anyone who has carried a lifeless frame over any distance will confirm. Thus lifting and lowering the deceased into a coffin becomes a task for more than one person and since my father's only other funeral colleague was a gravedigger who was more often out of town fencing or working in a shearing shed, finding someone quickly to help wasn't always easy.

To be fair, it wasn't a job for everyone. In some cases, a relative of the deceased would offer to help but then there were other occasions when next of kin didn't even want to enter the same room as the deceased, let alone assist in lifting the body into a wooden box.

That was how it came to be that, largely for insurance purposes, the first words uttered by my father—after the knock on the door or the telephone brought news of another entrant in the Pearly Gate Stakes—were: 'Find Sausage for me.'

Sometimes that was easier said than done. Occasionally there was suspicion that Sausage might have heard about the event beforehand and was staying out of sight because, despite the lure of extra drinking money, handling dead bodies was not high on Sausage Jamison's list of preferred odd jobs.

My father thought this was strange, as Sausage had no qualms about being in close contact with other aspects of the trade, a fact that was brought home to him and Nace Kane late one night when they arrived home from their weekly card game at the RSL to find Sausage asleep in one of the coffins in the back room. My father claimed Nace got a bigger fright than he did when Sausage's bleary-eyed countenance appeared above the edge of the coffin, complaining about them making too much noise. Before they could answer him the head disappeared and Sausage was fast asleep again.

Generally though, the standard procedure for finding Sausage began with visits to each of the three hotels and the RSL club to quiz drinkers about his whereabouts. If that failed, it was straight to the police station. Sausage and the Holbrook constabulary, aided and abetted by the justice system, had what could be called a special relationship.

Police stations in country towns aren't much different to other houses in the community in their requirements for lawns to be mowed, wood to be chopped in the winter months or gardens to be tended. In Holbrook's case Sausage completed these tasks admirably, since he was often to be found a little worse for wear and sleeping on the footpath, and would wake up to find himself in the cell behind the police residence. It wasn't a case of heavy handedness by the police, simply an opportunity to get him off the street and enable him to dry out for a while. The fact that there were a few chores to be done around the police station and residence could easily be regarded as a coincidence.

Of course a charge would have to be laid—usually something relating vaguely to vagrancy or to do with being drunk in a public place—and the next Holbrook court day would see a fine of ten shillings or three to four days in the lockup for Sausage; it depended on just how many chores needed doing around the police station and residence, as the payment of a ten-shilling fine was hardly an option for Sausage. Anyway, the way Sausage saw it there was no point wasting that sort of money on freedom, even if he did have the funds. And besides, penal servitude as the guest of the police was rarely a tough experience for Sausage; the police station was directly opposite the Bottom Pub and it was the Bottom Pub that provided the meals for anyone unfortunate enough to find themselves in a cell.

So the day or two that substituted for the ten-shilling fine would be spent tidying the paths or weeding the gardens until it came time for Sausage to undertake his last chore of the day—collecting his own meal from the Bottom Pub. He'd wander across the road with enough time to down a beer or two before returning to the cell with his hot meal.

It was all pretty civilised and relaxed, with three good meals a day and a warm bed; there was even some doubt about whether the police bothered to lock his cell at night. Certainly there was never any problem letting Sausage out early to help the local undertaker overcome a shortage of manpower. Occasionally, Dad would organise for him to assist Kelly with the gravedigging duties if Kelly was running behind time. But this was not something Kelly O'Brien liked, and he often complained that Sausage had trouble doing his fair share of the work.

The two nearly came to blows one afternoon. They'd been working their routine for almost an hour, each taking a turn to rest and have a swig or two of wine under a nearby gum tree while the other dug for a couple of feet. Kelly's suspicions that Sausage may not have been pulling his weight were confirmed when Sausage jumped out of the grave and announced it was now Kelly's turn.

The light may have been fading but Kelly could tell by looking into the hole that only a small amount of earth had been excavated during Sausage's shift. It was the last straw for Kelly.

'Soss, you're a bludger,' he levelled at his co-worker. 'If you've dug what you said you have then this bloody grave's got a rising bottom.'

'What do you mean Kelly,' responded Sausage, with just a hint of hurt in his voice.

'You've been in there for ten bloody minutes and by the look of the amount you've dug, all you've been doing down there is making a lot of noise with the shovel.'

Sausage opened his mouth to argue but Kelly, his annoyance becoming more obvious by the second, cut him short. 'Get to buggery out of the place,' Kelly warned, 'before I punch you in the bloody nose. I'll finish it myself.'

An obviously offended Sausage told my father later he could still hear Kelly shouting after him as he reached the other side of the cemetery fence.

Despite Kelly's critical assessment of Sausage's willingness to pull his weight, my father continued to use Sausage. It wasn't long, though, before they too came to a parting of the ways, although when it happened it turned out to be Sausage who initiated the break.

Late one morning, Dad asked Soss to accompany him to the morgue to help lift the body of a shearer into the coffin, so that he could set things up for the funeral the next day. Now the Holbrook morgue wasn't the most salubrious of places, simply a tin shed containing a wooden slab off to one side of the Holbrook Hospital on the eastern fringe of town. Needless to say, due to the heat, my father dreaded having anything to do with the building in the summer months.

Once they were inside they placed the casket on the floor and, with Soss at the feet end, slid the deceased towards the edge of the slab. They took the body's weight and were lowering him into the box, when, doubtless due to air forced out by the body's movement, from out of the shearer came a low rumbling sound, something like a dull groan. Sausage's face immediately creased in horror, fear doubtless crossing his mind at the thought that the shearer had been prematurely placed on the slab. Before my father could react, Soss had dropped his end of the corpse, sending the lower part of the torso crashing into the coffin. He bolted for the door, leaving a very agitated and red-faced country undertaker holding the heavy end of the shearer and screaming obscenities at Sausage's back. Dad's now former assistant half-walked and half-ran towards the hospital gate.

After that, Dad got Dave Preston, the caretaker at the shire hall, to help. Nuggety Dave was only around five foot six in height but he proved a much steadier working companion than Sausage. And he was far easier to find when needed, having a regular job and never needing to spend some of his time doing the gardens at the police residence. But even Dave's reliability was tested the night they went to pick up the dead wino from the Guvvy Dam.

Guvvy Dam was the local shorthand description for the government dam, which sat in the middle of several acres of low-lying swamp country near the railway station at the northern end of town. It had been used in the old days to supply water to the trains running from Holbrook to join the main Sydney–Melbourne line at Culcairn.

It had been years since the trains operated, so few people had any reason to go near the Guvvy Dam. The only building of any note along the expanse of the swamp was a corrugated iron shack, which had long been claimed by two local winos who'd decided it might be just good enough to provide a roof over their heads. And it wasn't all that far from the Top Pub, where they could spend the greater part of the day sitting on the footpath under the pub verandah testing the generosity of arriving patrons. It seemed to work too, as late most afternoons they could be seen heading homewards down the gravel stretch towards the Guvvy Dam each with a bottle in a brown paper bag under their arm.

The daily ritual had become very accepted. It wasn't until one of the customers at the Top Pub commented he hadn't seen either of the winos for a few days that someone rang the police. They went to the hut to find one of them wouldn't be making the trip down the gravel road any more. His companion was nowhere to be seen. It was late in the afternoon when my mother took the call from the police to say they needed Dad to pick up the body, but he'd taken a couple of shearers out to a property on the Wagga Road. She said she would pass on the message as soon as he returned.

Unfortunately it was well after dark when my mother realised that Dad would have to pass—and therefore stop at—the Top Pub on the way back from the Wagga Road job. So by the time she tracked him down he was well into a drinking session with a few of his mates and argued it was too late in the day to worry about picking up the body. But Mum said the police insisted it be done immediately, as the shed didn't have a door and all sorts of dreadful things could happen with animals roaming the swamp. Anyway, she'd already arranged for Dave Preston to give Dad a hand.

By the time Dave and Dad loaded a spare casket into the back of the Essex and reached the edge of the swamp it was almost nine o'clock and they realised they had a problem. In the dull glow of the old hearse's headlights they could see that, thanks to recent rain, the swamp itself was covered in several inches of water and there was no way the Essex could negotiate it without getting bogged. Added to that, the moment the headlights were turned off they were pitched into total darkness and all they could make out were the eerie shapes of the swamp's gum trees silhouetted against the thin glow of the town lights a quarter of a mile away.

Dave had brought his torch but by the time they argued about which actual direction the hut was in and had come to the conclusion they'd have to carry the coffin in by hand, what was left of the torch batteries provided little more than a yellow gleam.

Within half a dozen steps into the swamp they were wading through water up to their ankles and conditions got steadily worse as, with little assistance from the torch, they stumbled across ground which alternated between water-filled cattle tracks and half-submerged logs. Finally the hut appeared before them, just a shadowy shape against the treeline. Dumping the coffin on the ground outside, they groped their way inside to be met by the stench of stale wine and the odour that comes from months of unwashed bodies and dirty clothes.

Thanks to what was left of the torch, Dave and Dad could just make out a lifeless body stretched out along a bunk on the far side of the hut. Wet and exhausted from the trek across the swamp, and not wishing to stay a second longer than necessary, they each grabbed an end. They had lifted the shape only six inches or so when my father felt one leg twitch, and from Dave's end came a groan loud enough to echo around the tin walls of the hut. As one, they let go of each end and without any help at all from the torch were both out the door in an instant.

Dave and Dad were several yards into the swamp again before they stopped and gathered themselves enough to re-enter the hut. There, they found their earlier prospect still stretched out on the floor where he'd landed. This time the torchlight also fell on a second shape, lying against the wall on the other side of the room. There were no twitches or groans as they gingerly manoeuvred the lifeless form around his still-prostrate colleague and out into the waiting coffin.

They were putting the lid on the coffin when Dad noticed a brand new pair of gumboots standing near the doorway, which at least helped ease his journey back through the swamp.

When they reached the hearse, Dave asked Dad if he was going to hand in the boots to the police. There was no way that was going to happen.

'They'll be handy to wear while washing the car,' he said. Obviously good gumboots, like good help, were hard to find.

14

The return of football

It's difficult to pinpoint the exact moment that football came back into the life of the country undertaker. Most likely it just crept in and inevitably swept Mick Eames up, simply because it was so much a part of the culture of a country town like Holbrook. Drought, floods, fire and even wars might come and go but football was always there—well, in Holbrook's case, Australian Rules football at least. While the high altar of such a religion might have been in Melbourne there was no doubting the passion in the parish known as the Albury and District League.

Despite its narrow window as a winter sport, football's interest and influence in a country town of the 1950s extended well beyond the actual season. A member of the community was more likely to be known and respected for his prowess on the football oval than for the fact that he was a gun shearer or a first-rate motor mechanic. The same could be said of the town itself, because the very status of a town in the Albury and District League was judged largely on its success or otherwise on a Saturday afternoon. This, in some cases at least, developed into a degree of inter-town rivalry which had whole communities squaring off against each other for the rest of the year, often spilling over into business and social relationships.

Often, the closer two towns were geographically or in size, the sharper the rivalry, and your ranking as part of the district was in large part measured by the number of premierships you had won. Of all eight teams in the Albury and District League, this was the way it was between Holbrook and Culcairn. Both about the same size, there was a stand-off between the two, like two small destroyers, both taking every opportunity to fire a status shell across the eighteen miles or so separating them. For its part, Culcairn sat smugly astride the main Sydney to Melbourne railway line as if such a location bore greater prestige than Holbrook's straddle of the Hume Highway. As Culcairn witnessed the long interstate express trains rumble through their town day and night, the people of Holbrook could sense their Culcairn counterparts sneering at the rapidly decaying tracks on the branch line which had previously run from Culcairn to Holbrook, as if yet another example of their loftier place in the scheme of things.

When it came to football the innuendos were many and brutal, heightened by the fact that Holbrook hadn't won a premiership for almost twenty years. That we'd missed out by only a point or two on several occasions didn't ease the pain, nor did the fact that it wasn't Culcairn who had most claim to the title but rather the tiny hamlet of Mangoplah, just to the north.

Surrounded by little more than a general store and a real estate agent, the local publican tired of polishing the A and D League premiership cups above the bar at the Mangoplah Hotel. With a small population and few people to choose from, somehow or other a team emerged from Mangoplah's surrounding farms every Saturday to carry away the flag. Nace Kane, who'd been a star player for Holbrook in his younger days, reckoned they came out of rabbit burrows every weekend. But wherever they came from no one begrudged Mangoplah its success. At least they played the game fairer than those buggers from Culcairn.

Holbrook's first training runs for the football season had only just started when Brian Brennan approached my father with an offer he couldn't refuse, partly to help solve a problem Brian had of his own. Brian Brennan was the personification of everything my father had always wanted to be as a footballer but had not been blessed with. Darkly handsome, he moved on the field with a feline grace and an anticipation which not only made him a favourite with Holbrook supporters but convinced the football club committee that he should be both captain and coach for the 1951 season.

Brian's problem, though, was that he couldn't do both, which was why he needed my father's help. A contract shearer, Brian spent much of every week out of town in district shearing sheds, which made it almost impossible for him to supervise any training sessions during the week. But he knew enough about my father's background to realise there might be a way around it.

'If you'll take on the job of coach, Mick, I'll take on the captain's job,' he suggested. Such a suggestion would have been music to my father's ears and he'd probably answered the question before Brian Brennan finished asking it. It wasn't long after, however, that a problem appeared.

It seemed that while Brian might be the favourite son of the Holbrook football fraternity, several on the club committee considered he'd acted outside his authority by offering the coaching job to my father before first running it past the committee.

The following few days were confused ones for my father. After all, to have some doubt thrown up about his involvement in a task he'd be willing to walk over broken glass for was something he found difficult to deal with. And the committee's deliberations on the issue were taking place over a few drinks at the RSL club, forcing him to avoid the club for fear of influencing the outcome to his disadvantage. So his relief was palpable when Brian called in the following week.

'I told them,' Brian said, 'there was no way I could be at training on Tuesdays and Thursdays, Mick, so they could take it or leave it. They've decided to take it.'

If my father thought that was the end of it then he was mistaken. It turned out that the lack of consultation issue had filtered down to some of the players, and only half of them turned up for the training session on the next Tuesday night. While my father was concerned, Brian

Brennan wasn't fazed, believing that most of the players loved the game too much to drag the issue out for too long. But even Brian started to take things seriously when a small group didn't turn up for the first practice match of the season, and a very annoyed captain arrived unexpectedly during training the following Tuesday.

'Okay, we're not going to cop this,' Brian told the assembled throng. 'You're either in or you're out, so make up your mind.'

When he came home that night, Dad told Mum there was a moment or two when he thought they might have to recruit Sausage Jamison or Digger O'Brien, the boundary umpire, to help make up the numbers. But apart from a few isolated grumbles that was the end of it. After that, it was simply a case of Holbrook Football Club's new coach following his captain's instructions during his absence.

'Run 'em up and down for six miles every Tuesday night,' Brian had instructed Dad, 'and a bit less on Thursday, and I'll do the rest.'

What my mother thought of this return to the bad old days of sweaty jockstraps and mud-caked football boots was hard to fathom; busy with her café, she appeared too preoccupied to worry. However she was probably relieved to some extent that, at least for a few hours two nights each week, her husband was absent from the RSL or the Top Pub. She even appeared to show tacit approval and became part of it when the Australian Café played host to the club's first pie night of the year. Ever the focused skipper, though, Brian Brennan was not going to let this initial largesse go to the players' heads, announcing at the start of the evening that there would be only one other pie night for the year, and then only if they made it to the finals.

As football teams go, Holbrook was a typical country side, consisting to a large extent of the sons of farming families. The Cottrell brothers made up four of the eighteen team members, which you might have thought would create some confusion among the Albury and District League officials. However, the parents of the two Heather brothers, both on the team, had gone one step further. They'd christened one son Harold and the other Harry.

On top of that there was Harold Breasley and his near namesake big Kevin Beazley, both of whom were destined to give my father some anxious moments as the season progressed. Big Kev played in the ruck and it soon became obvious that, as my father put it, he 'would rather a fight than a feed', a tendency often provoked by an opposing team who could see significant advantages in having the big man out of the side for a week or two.

Both big Kev and Harold almost fell victim to provocation in the first game against Wagga. They came through unscathed, however, and Holbrook won, with eight of the thirteen goals being kicked by Tommy Jones, the rover. My father was beside himself with joy, but his captain saw it differently.

'We'd have won by a bloody lot more if we could kick straight,' said Brian, in an obvious reference to the eighteen points which also decorated the scoreboard.

But there were ominous signs as, by the time the team had gathered for the customary post-match drinks at the Middle Pub word was already in that arch enemies Culcairn had beaten Henty, another team in the League, by a massive twenty-four goals—the highest recorded score in the Albury and District League since way back early in the century.

'Such a development so early in the season calls for serious steps to be taken,' said Brian Brennan before he and my father parted company that evening.

'Make 'em run that six miles harder,' continued Brian. And then, to my father's horror, he added, 'And make sure no one has a drink after Tuesday night.'

There were any number of things my father would sacrifice for football, but going without a drink wasn't one of them. Even in his days playing for Wodonga and as captain and coach of South Albury he'd only once ever had to face the prospect of limiting his drinking. And that was only when his brother Jack had placed a ban on drinking at Wodonga, and then only between Thursday night and Saturday's match.

He might have been tempted to suggest to his captain that as non-playing coach he should be exempt from such a ruling. But his reluctance to do so, or so he explained to my mother, had something to do with his requirement to set an example for his players. It was more likely, though, that given the earlier dissension over his appointment as coach, he wasn't going to give the committee any excuse to revisit that issue. He'd just have to find a way around it.

Initially, my father's return to something of a fitness regime momentarily distracted him from drinking, and it must have proved a benefit when he was suddenly selected to play in the forward pocket when two of the players failed to return from injury in time for the match against The Rock. It was the first time he'd pulled on a team guernsey in anger since his days with South Albury. You could tell he was proud of it when he cut out the clipping naming the team in the *Border Morning Mail* that week, along with the notation for players to wear 'white knicks', signifying it was an 'away' game and instructions on what the transport arrangements were to be.

Often, at least for some players, getting to an away game was a bit of an exercise in its own right. Not everyone had a car in those days and any who did were asked to pool to carry the senior players and club officials. The A70 Austin was always pressed into service while the Cottrell boys and the other farmers would drive their own utes. The remainder followed the *Border Morning Mail*'s instructions to meet outside the post office in the main street at 12.30 p.m. with the prospect of travelling on the back of Hec McKinley's 1942 tray-body truck. Hec was captain of Holbrook's second eighteen and used the Chev to cart wood during the week. For its Saturday role he'd place a few long wooden stools on the tray and erect a tarpaulin over them to provide at least some protection for the players. But even then the journey home from an away match on a cold winter's night, while trying to stay upright on wobbly stools, was not for the faint hearted.

Holbrook easily won the game against The Rock. Brian Brennan credited this to his revised coaching regime, assisted marginally by the two goals kicked by a resurgent Mick Eames in the forward pocket. But the other news was not good, with Culcairn having another equally easy win over the previous year's premiers, Mangoplah, who were to be our next opponents.

The match against Mangoplah turned out to be a cracker. Holbrook began to pull away in the second quarter despite the fact that Charlie Craig, local builder and star full forward, was not kicking straight. Then, much to my father's initial concern, Charlie changed tactics at the start of the second half.

It was general practice in Holbrook that many of the same players who strapped on the boots for the Aussie Rules team on Saturday also kitted up on Sunday for the Holbrook rugby league team. It was a practice which did not sit easily with coach Mick Eames, brought up to believe there was only one code of football and any other should not be allowed to contaminate it. But he'd had to live with the consequences of team members playing two codes, particularly when someone like big Kev Beazley would take out an opposing player with a bone-crushing tackle and thereby give away a free kick, which would instantly be followed by a shout from coach Eames from the boundary: 'For Christ's sake Kevin, remember which day it is.'

Thus it was at Mangoplah that Charlie Craig, frustrated at missing too many shots at goal with his punt kicks, suddenly reverted to his Sunday role and started to gouge the turf with the heel of his boot and then prop the ball on the resultant mound for a place kick. Aghast at such a sacrilegious act, my father yelled at Brennan to stop him. But Brian knew better and anyway it was too late as, to Holbrook's delight, the kick went straight through the middle. Charlie, filled with new-found confidence, kicked four more the same way to seal victory and lift morale considerably for the much anticipated match against Culcairn at Holbrook the next week.

As usually happened when the two protagonists met, there was a build-up of tension before the game. This time it was heightened by Culcairn arriving at the ground early and lodging a complaint about the surface, which they claimed was 'overgrassed' and would therefore make fast football, their acknowledged trademark, out of the question. As it turned out, however, it made no difference. Holbrook's form of the previous week deserted them, along with Charlie Craig's place kicks, and Holbrook went down by three goals after kicking an appalling fifteen points.

Things didn't improve the next week, when Holbrook suffered defeat at the hands of Wagga. It wasn't easy to take the second loss in a row, not least because of an incident that occurred late in the final quarter which almost resulted in coach Eames' football season coming to a premature end at the hands of Albury and District League officialdom.

It all started quite innocently when the team arrived at Wagga's Bolton Park to be told that one of the boundary umpires hadn't turned up. There was a huddle among the players and officials and it turned out that the only person available and fit enough to do the job was the Holbrook coach. So just before the bell sounded for the opening quarter, there was my father running onto the ground in the white shorts and shirt attire of the boundary umpire. Surprisingly, perhaps, but doubtless due to the extra impetus of the training regime, he stayed up with the play, his bandy legs pumping like pistons as he scurried around the boundary, enthusiastically waving his white handkerchief whenever the ball went over the line.

All went well until the final quarter when, with Wagga starting to draw away, the ball went out of bounds near Holbrook's forward pocket. Anyone watching closely would probably have noticed the coach-turned-boundary umpire keeping more than a boundary umpire's eye on the scoreboard as he grabbed the ball. He seemed quite deliberate as he walked back to the boundary line and, in the instant before turning his back to throw the ball back over his head and into play, he appeared to take a long, hard look at where Brian Brennan was off to one side and close to the goal posts. Sure enough, the throw-in speared sharply off to the left of the waiting ruckmen, falling right into the arms of one B. Brennan, who turned quickly onto his left foot and snapped for goal. He missed.

Before anyone could react, Holbrook's substitute boundary umpire, in what must have been a reflex action, fixed his errant captain with a piercing stare and, hands planted firmly on hips, shouted: 'You silly bastard. You want me to kick the bloody thing for you as well!'

Unfortunately, it wasn't only the group of Wagga supporters on the fence who heard him. The match umpire raced in and, no doubt fearing a near-riot among the spectators, pointed in the direction of the change sheds and ordered a very guilty looking boundary umpire off the field of play, shouting after him for all to hear that if he ever saw him running the boundary again he'd make sure he was banned for life.

Despite several losses on the trot, by the time we'd reached the second round of the home-and-away games it was apparent that Holbrook was still in with a chance at the finals. Things were going according to plan in the renewed football life of Mick Eames, coach of the Holbrook football team. Unfortunately the same could not always be said for the activities of Mick Eames, country undertaker.

It all had something to do with snakes.

15

Snakes are unpredictable buggers

I realise you could never call them endearing creatures but I don't know why my father disliked snakes so much. Maybe it was a result of growing up in South Albury, only a few yards from river flats which stretched from the Eames family home all the way to the Murray River, the tufts of grass and low scrub forming a natural habitat for reptiles.

Whatever the reason, killing snakes was second nature to my father and it appeared that it was only the method of doing it that created any interest. Since there was a .22 rifle in the house, it was the norm to get as close as you could to the slithering reptile and display your accuracy by shooting it in the head. Hitting it anywhere else apparently wasn't anything to brag about. But when it came to dispatching them via unconventional methods, none of the brothers could match Uncle George.

In the time George had spent on the timber trucks he'd picked up the ability to stealthily approach a snake from behind, snatch it by the tail and in one brisk, sweeping motion flick it as you would crack a whip, breaking its back in the process. There's no record of any of the other brothers attempting a similar method of dispatch (presumably out of fear of what might happen if the 'whip' didn't crack at the first attempt) so they probably shrugged off George's talent by silently acknowledging he'd be the only one silly enough to try. After all, none of the others was ever likely to jump into the boxing ring with the Alabama Kid.

In my father's case, it appeared that the only good snake was a dead one, an attitude that was hardened by what happened that day at the cemetery which had become his nemesis—Woomargama.

I often wondered why cemeteries like the one at Woomargama were placed on a hillside. Not that Woomargama's was on much of a hill: it was just sloping ground running down to the west on the northern edge of the town. But it was a hill nonetheless, the same damn hill that had caused the Essex's wheels to slip the day the coffin wouldn't fit. Maybe someone way back had the idea that the dead needed a view or should be able to look down on those left behind, or that the latter should be forced to look up at the dead in respect. My mother was convinced this seeking of the high ground was a religious thing, part of a plan by the various churches who, she always claimed, looked for the high ground, and the positioning of cemeteries was a spin off from that. 'The Catholics are the worst,' she would say, never failing to point out the position of the Catholic church as we drove through a country town. 'Look, there's the Catholic church. They've got the top of the hill again.'

Woomargama cemetery's gentle slope hadn't helped much the last time we'd been there, the day it had been raining, but at least on this occasion the weather was dry and hot. As usual, despite the small size of the town, a large crowd could be expected to attend. Like tiny Mangoplah when it came to producing footballers, no one quite knew where all the mourners came from at Woomargama.

Kelly had left Holbrook the afternoon before to get a head start on the grave and had managed to complete it before nightfall. So it had only been necessary for him to return to the cemetery shortly before the hearse's arrival to be ready for the filling-in process. Sure enough, there he was, having taken up his customary position partly out of sight behind a small tree on the back edge of the cemetery.

Kelly was the first thing my father looked for when he approached any cemetery. The presence of the parson, number of cars, or the number of mourners was of little initial interest to him, but the status of Kelly O'Brien was critical. The moment the cemetery came into sight my father's eyes would scan across the headstones and around the gum trees for Kelly. You could see the relief in Dad's face once he saw that Kelly was well away from the gravesite, which meant he could dismiss the ever-present dread of any country undertaker doing an out-of-town job—how to handle a situation where, out of contact with your gravedigger for hours beforehand, you arrive leading a half-mile long convoy of mourners to find your gravedigger had struck an obstinate chunk of rock and is still digging.

But today was fine, and by this time, with a brace of funerals under their belt, Kelly and my father had few reasons to exchange chatter at the site. As usual it was simply a cursory nod from Kelly in my father's direction when their eyes met to confirm that all was in order. Little else was needed. The big-city procedure of surrounding the grave with a mat of artificial turf and the setting up of some mechanical device to assist in the lowering of the coffin had not yet made it into the operations manual of my father. So it took only a minute or two of scrambling around the dirt mound beside the grave to jam the two four-by-two boards firmly across the opening, ready to receive the casket.

Everything was going pretty well. The reverend had completed his solemn entreaties and my father was reaching down to slip the four-by-twos out, when the deceased's brother, a tall man in his sixties in the front row of the mourners, stepped forward and looked down into the hole. Why he did that, no one would ever know, but the thought crossed my mind that maybe he was at the last funeral my father did at Woomargama and was checking to see if the hole was wide enough for the coffin to fit. When he spoke it had the effect of a rifle shot in the silence.

'There's a snake in that grave. We can't bury her with that there.'

And there was a snake there all right, a four-foot brown. You could tell from the look on my father's face that things were unravelling fast, as murmurs came from the crowd and those at the back began to shuffle forward to have a look for themselves. With the pallbearers still waiting on the end of the straps to take the weight, father had obviously decided we'd passed the point of no return to worry much about a snake. So, still crouched with one hand on the end of a four-by-two he looked directly up into the eyes of the tall man and muttered something about the snake not doing her any harm.

There followed a brief argument which led to my father's fall-back position, which was to suggest that perhaps the mourners should all toddle off and leave him to fix the problem. But Relative Number One was having none of it. His tone of voice had sharpened by the time he pointed out quite forcibly that there was no way he was going to leave 'until she's been appropriately laid to rest'.

My father must have derived some minor satisfaction in seeing small groups of mourners start to wander off. There was, however, no mistaking the annoyance in the brisk wave of his hand which directed the pallbearers to move the casket to the side of the grave, and his terse command for Kelly to come out from behind the tree. With those that remained looking on, my father and Kelly—by now prostrate on the ground beside the grave—proceeded to take it in turns to attack the snake with Kelly's shovel and a crowbar.

Now, I don't know whether many of you have seen a four-foot brown snake at the bottom of a six-foot hole but I can guarantee the snake had no sense of humour. And

I could see its point. It had probably been slithering down a well-worn track on that hillside for years, to find one morning that someone had suddenly dug a hole across its path. Kelly O'Brien must have been quietly thanking his lucky stars he hadn't been still digging when the snake had arrived.

It seemed to take an age to kill the snake. The more times the shovel descended towards it, the angrier it became, whipping backwards and forwards around the bottom of the grave until Kelly managed to strike the fatal blow, leaving two halves in the place of one.

Exhausted from the effort and with his dark suit covered in dirt, my father rose off his stomach. With a resigned wave of his hand he beckoned the pallbearers forward again, just as Relative Number One pointed out that someone should do the gracious thing and remove the remains of the reptile before the casket was lowered. The glare in my father's eyes, however, made it quite clear there was no chance of that happening, the message being that if Relative Number One wanted the snake retrieved from the bottom of the grave then he could do so himself. As Kelly moved back behind his tree, the reverend, obviously deeming it wise to start again, repeated his words of departure until, in the presence of Relative Number One and the dozen or so mourners who were left, the lady was duly returned to nature, albeit with a little uninvited company.

The cemetery had hardly been deserted for more than a minute or so when my father and Kelly started to argue about who was to blame, with my father asserting that Kelly should have checked the grave properly before the funeral cortege arrived. Kelly for his part was adamant that he had done so and hadn't noticed the snake—but even if he had he would not have done anything about it, as he couldn't see it doing a dead person in a coffin any harm.

Around and around the argument went with neither of them prepared to give an inch, and I think that might have been when my father decided he'd bide his time and get his own back.

16

Reptilian revenge

The experience at Woomargama cemetery confirmed in my father's mind the righteousness of killing any snake which came into his field of vision. And the time he spent at the wheel of the taxi on country roads provided him with ample opportunity to indulge his passion.

Whether the surface was bitumen or gravel, his practised eye could spot a snake crossing the road from several hundred yards away, allowing him plenty of time to line up the unfortunate reptile as it wriggled towards the safety of the road verge. A second or two before it slipped out of sight under the front of the car, he would slam on the brakes, using the skidding rear wheels to rid Mick Eames' patch of earth of yet another unnecessary evil. It was something of a cold, remote method of execution, followed by a brief stop and quick inspection to confirm his handiwork had achieved the desired result.

It made no difference whether the taxi was carrying a load of paying passengers or Dad was on his own. No one ever complained and no one ever seemed to mind him boasting about it, particularly his mates at the Top Pub who all seemed to consider it a worthwhile talent to acknowledge.

My father's planned revenge for the snake in the grave at Woomargama came together several weeks after the funeral, when he was returning from a job out on the Jingellic Road. He spotted a big four-footer scurrying across the gravel road in front of him. There was a quick realignment of direction, a vicious stamp on the brake pedal and then one very dead-looking red-bellied black lying in the middle of the road behind the car. Never had my father shown the slightest inclination to touch even a dead snake but on this occasion his anticipation of the look on Kelly O'Brien's face must have momentarily over-ridden his abhorrence for the creatures. It was with trembling hands that he emptied the car jack and tools from the hessian bag in the boot and gingerly lifted the snake by the tail into the bag.

There were only five or six men drinking in the bar when Dad arrived at the Top Pub around eleven in the morning the same day. As he'd predicted, Kelly was there, sitting at one end talking to Jack Spurr, the jovial, rotund barman. Nonchalantly dropping the bag on the floor at his feet, he waited while Kelly ordered him a beer. They chatted for a while. Then, obviously judging that his victim was suitably relaxed, Dad reached down, picked up the bag and in one sweeping motion emptied its contents on the bar between him and Kelly.

What happened next taught Mick Eames, practical joker, a lesson no one would ever let him forget. Instead of a lifeless body hitting the bar top, one very much alive red-bellied black uncoiled itself and slithered along the top of the counter for a few feet, before slipping over the edge and dropping the three or four feet into the ash tray-cum-footrest running the length of the bar at floor level. The small group of drinkers at the other end of the bar appeared momentarily stunned then started to shuffle slowly back on their stools. But according to Jack Spurr there was nothing slow about my father's reaction.

Whether it was the surprise of seeing the snake move along the bar or the realisation that he'd in fact picked up a live snake off the road and placed it in the bag, no one could say, but it took only a second or two for my father to react. There was a clatter as his stool crashed to the floor and in an instant he was gone through the side door and out onto the footpath, as far as possible from the red-bellied black.

As for Kelly O'Brien, according to the story Jack Spurr would tell to my father's deep embarrassment for years to come, the old bushman just sat there, folded arms resting on the edge of the bar, a half grin on his face as he watched the snake slide off the counter onto the floor. Kelly stayed that way until Spurr arrived back with a shovel from the shed at the back of the pub. Then he slipped quietly off his stool, took the spade from Spurr and dispatched the unfortunate reptile on the footpath. By this time, Spurr would recount at every available opportunity, my father was nowhere to be seen.

17

The premiership

It was probably fortunate that no one died at either Holbrook or Woomargama in the last six weeks of the 1951 football season, as I doubt whether the country undertaker would have had enough time to bury them.

Once Holbrook made it into the final, the prospect of breaking a twenty-year premiership drought became all-consuming. Even my mother seemed to be enjoying it. Not that she had much option; the mere act of opening the café door of a morning to sweep the footpath usually resulted in someone appearing to discuss our chances.

Meanwhile, with his captain still out of town during the week on shearing commitments, my father was relishing his pivotal role in the twice-weekly training sessions, strategy discussions with members of the committee and the all-important duck raffle.

Duck or chook raffles were an essential part of running a country football club like Holbrook and were used to raise funds for the payment of the umpires for the league's

Saturday matches. Holbrook's raffle was held at the Middle Pub after training every Tuesday night, largely because the Middle Pub was the closest one to the Holbrook football ground where training was held and Tuesday happened to be the last night the players were permitted to have a drink under Brian Brennan's 'no alcohol' edict. Not that my father was too concerned about the latter requirement; so far no one had noticed that he'd managed to get around the ban by parking his car out of sight around the back of the hotel on the remaining nights of the week, arranging for the barman to bring the drinks out to him in the kitchen of the publican's house at the rear. It was lonely drinking, but at least it was drinking.

There was a degree of showmanship involved in conducting the raffle and my father's gregarious nature made him a natural for playing a prominent part. He ran the raffle with the club's unofficial boundary umpire, Digger O'Brien—no relation to Holbrook's favourite gravedigger but, along with Brian Brennan, a local shearing contractor. Digger and Brian were good mates and not only worked together in the sheds but Brian was also a boarder at Digger's wife's place when he was in town at weekends.

The duck raffle night was always a big drawcard at the Middle Pub and the bar was often packed to capacity as people watched Digger and my father shouting and cajoling, even embarrassing the patrons until a whole two books of tickets were sold. Probably due to sales becoming easier as more alcohol was consumed, no one seemed to bother much about the fact that the draw for the raffle never took place on the Tuesday night but would be announced later in the week.

Usually, by the time the following Tuesday night raffle came around someone would ask, 'Who won last week, Digger?'

Invariably the answer was something like, 'A bloke from Mullengandra. He bought the ticket from Mick during the week.' Or 'A transport driver on his way through. We sold him the ticket at the Top Pub.'

By that time this week's ticket-selling binge was in full swing and no one seemed to bother much that the winner never came from among the throng at the Middle Pub, and anyway, it was all for a good cause.

By the time Wagga beat Mangoplah to win the first semi-final, Holbrook's colours of green and gold were appearing in shop windows the length of the main street. Small groups of locals were even braving the chilly night at training to watch my father and Brennan, who was now driving into town after shearing every Tuesday and Thursday, put the players through their paces as they prepared to meet Culcairn in the second semi-final at Mangoplah.

When Saturday finally came there were not only heightened expectations at Holbrook but it turned out to be the first time an event such as a final had been played at tiny Mangoplah. They even had to knock down a fence at the ground to provide extra parking. Other parts of the boundary were still a problem, however, as a wayward kick out of bounds over the left side of the ground meant someone had to retrieve the ball from the waters of Bourke's Creek a few yards away.

If stars were to be made that day it was big Kev Beazley's turn to shine as he dominated the ruck, drove the ball forward to create opportunities for Brennan and Charlie Craig to score and even booted a goal from a place kick himself. By the time the team arrived back in town on Hec McKinley's truck everyone had heard the news that we were in the grand final, to play the winner of the Culcairn–Wagga clash the following week. Or so we all thought. In fact, the next Saturday one point separated the two teams with only minutes to play when Culcairn scored to draw the match. So another week had to pass before Culcairn, showing some alarming form the second time around, staked their claim to a grand final berth.

So the two arch rivals, who had joined the A and D League at the same time forty-three years before, and rarely in the time since had said anything nice about each other, would meet at Mangoplah.

We didn't see much of my father that week but the *Border Morning Mail* told its readers that 'coach Mick Eames is pleased with his team's form and is confident of beating Culcairn', which wasn't strictly true. In the rare occasions he came home between meetings and training sessions my father made no secret of his fear that the extra week's break as a result of the Culcairn–Wagga draw match had taken its toll on the players. He'd even organised an extra training game against an Albury team to make up for it.

When the umpire bounced the ball at 2.20 p.m. at Mangoplah on Saturday, 1 September 1951 it appeared my father's fears might have been justified. Culcairn surged to an eighteen-point lead at quarter time and there was more than the usual tension in the pep talk Brennan gave the team as they prepared to kick the other way.

But it worked. Holbrook came back with a vengeance, took control of the game and, as the *Border Mail* would later report, cut Culcairn to ribbons for the following two quarters, going into the final quarter forty-five points in front. Culcairn managed to peg back the score a little in the final quarter but Holbrook's defence held, and the flag was ours by twenty-nine points.

When the final bell sounded my father was standing inside the boundary fence in front of a clutch of Holbrook supporters. There was a shout, 'It's ours!' which could be heard above the roar of the rest of the crowd as he flung his arms in the air and bounded towards the centre of the ground where the players were already converging on Brian Brennan. Unfortunately he'd had the car keys in his hand and they soared back over his head into the crowd, and my mother ran off to retrieve them.

With hundreds swamping Mangoplah for the final it was almost impossible for the local pub to cope. It was late that night before Hec McKinley's truck pulled up outside the café and I heard George Cottrell's voice shouting, 'Where's the cockroach?', the player's nickname for their coach. Suddenly my father was gone again and we didn't see him until late the following day when he arrived home to announce there was a move to have the Brennan–Eames combination repeat the effort for the following year.

But the post-victory euphoria hadn't overcome the lingering effect of the early troubles with the committee, particularly in the eyes of the Holbrook captain.

'We've won the premiership and rubbed their noses in it Mick,' said Brian. 'Let's leave it at that.'

And they did leave it at that. Despite his love of the game, my father seemed content with the decision. After all, retiring at the top was not something he was used to.

As for the duck raffle: on the Sunday night after their grand final victory, Brennan, Digger O'Brien and big Kev Beazley sat down to a sumptuous roast duck dinner at Mrs O'Brien's boarding house. Brennan couldn't help asking where she got the ducks from.

'Oh, Digger and Mick keep them in the freezer every week and they said we might as well use them. They reckon they'll have to get a fresh pair for next year, anyway.'

18

Water holes and watering holes

Country towns drop into a void after the football season. The void is there because you realise pretty quickly that football training did a lot to fill the short winter days during the week, then wrapped you up for the weekend with the intensity of the lead-up to Saturday's game and the post mortem on Sundays. But there were signs even a week or so after the celebrations in Holbrook were over that the abyss would be even deeper for the town at the end of the 1951 season.

Thus it took the advent of the summer months to expose the shortcomings that come with living in the country, shortcomings which substitute sports like cricket or tennis have difficulty replacing. Sportspeople dressed in white never seemed to rate like footballers, with the result that even the back pages of the *Border Morning Mail* lacked any major attraction and there was no way a duck raffle for the cricket club would ever pack the bar at the Middle Pub.

Summer's dry, aching heat, stirred occasionally by hot winds from the north-west, brings other things to think about. Farmers don't talk much about it, but they worry about the wind and the sun, and the grass that has now dried from green to a light brown. Although they don't say it out loud, they're concerned about the city folk passing through on the highways—the farmers realise what a cigarette butt thrown carelessly out a car window can do. So they keep their water tanks and their firefighting Furphys full and toss frequent glances at the horizon for any telltale sliver of smoke.

Water is on the minds of the townsfolk too, but for a different reason. In their case it's more about the fact that there's nowhere to swim because the Ten Mile Creek, which splits the town in half under the bridge across the highway, has become a series of shallow, sad-looking water holes which themselves soon disappear altogether into a sinew of grey, sandy banks.

As summer progresses the preoccupation with swimming becomes almost obsessive. In Holbrook's case there are only two alternatives, both beyond reach of your bicycle or your legs if your parents don't have a car.

The closest was Billabong Creek which, unlike the Ten Mile, managed to retain a deep water hole for most of the summer. And although still around eighteen miles north of the town along the Hume Highway, it had the advantage, at least in the case of the Eames family, of being close to the Billabong Pub.

Even though we owned a taxi, Billabong Creek might have been out of reach of the Eameses were it not for the fact that pubs fell into two categories with my father, both of equal importance in the scheme of things. In the first category there were the 'essential' pubs, those which either formed part of his daily life in Holbrook itself or played an integral positioning role in the operation of the taxi service. In other words, they were en route between Dad's departure point and wherever he was going at the time. Those in the second category were the 'convenience' pubs, which had more to do with the way things were in the bush when it came to recreational activities (largely whether you could combine some family opportunity with the close proximity of a drinking establishment). Fortunately the Billabong pub fell into both categories, being midway between any taxi task involving Holbrook and Tarcutta, or when recreationally convenient, swimming on a hot summer weekend.

Billabong didn't really exist as a town—there was just the pub, an old, low level timber building jammed between a clutch of gum trees and several decaying water tanks a hundred yards or so off the highway. It was the domain of the Quinlan family and, for my mother at least—who'd been brought up to believe that most hotels were a licence to print money—the Billabong was something of an enigma. Indeed, she could occasionally be heard to wonder how the Quinlans made a living as there were only ever one or two drinkers in the bar, leading her to question where the drinkers came from as there wasn't another building in sight for miles around. Certainly, back in the days when Kelly O'Brien and his mate Gordon McLaurin were clearing land and droving cattle the Billabong was never short of customers. But these days it seemed to survive on weekend business, thanks to a species known in the trade as the 'bona fide traveller'. This was a gentleman who could be served a drink provided he had travelled more than twenty-five miles from his place of residence. In Holbrook's case the distance separating the two fell short of the required level, but there was obviously a little elasticity built into the requirement, even as far as the police were concerned.

Dad was there one Sunday when three police from the Wagga Flying Squad called in for a drink on their way back from raiding the Top Pub in Holbrook. Everyone in the bar was nervous until they got up to leave. As the first one reached the door he turned to Jack Quinlan, who was serving behind the bar, and said, 'I hope all these buggers are bona fide.'

'Bloody oath they are,' replied Jack, sounding as if he'd been offended by the question.

The policeman gave a knowing smile and walked to his car.

Thus, while Mum kept the café going on a Sunday, my father would frequently adopt a generous tone of voice and announce: 'I think I'll take the kids for a swim, Ed.' My brother Pete and I would be bundled into the car, then dropped off to spend the afternoon jumping off the four-foot bank into the stagnant brown water of the

Billabong until darkness approached and Dad decided it was time to collect us and drive home.

I often wondered what they found to talk about for all those hours in the bar of the Billabong. But I guess there was always the lack of rain, the price of beer and cigarettes, the fact that there'll never be another Don Bradman and, of course, the approaching football season. Politics would have come into it occasionally and it wouldn't have taken long for my father to establish his own position on that issue. Bob Menzies, with his cultured voice and double-breasted suits presented just the image you needed to lead a country like Australia. Now there was someone who obviously knew the value of the wool on the sheep's back and who could also keep those foreigners at bay. Though I doubt that the latter subject would have been raised too often at the Billabong; that was more likely to occur at home over lunch on Saturday.

At those lunches, you always knew something profound was coming when two things happened simultaneously: the *Border Morning Mail* was thrust forward several inches towards the centre of the table, accompanied by a short grunt.

'We need to watch it,' my father would say, his face over the top of the newspaper showing serious concern. 'I wouldn't trust that Sockarino bastard as far as I could kick him.'

My father might not have been a great student of world affairs but the *Border Morning Mail* conveyed enough information to allow him to form some definite opinions about who were the good and the bad guys in our part of the world.

'His mob will be in this place in a flash it he gets the chance.'

It usually fell to my mother to quietly adjust his target. 'Tidge, I don't think his name's Sockarino. It's Sukarno, or something like that,' she would say, couching her correction in such a way as to limit any embarrassment to Dad, while at the same time rescuing the butter dish from beneath the edge of the flattened newspaper.

'I don't give a bugger what his bloody name is. He's got us in his sights and we need to keep the bastard right where he is.'

My mother would quickly realise the futility of any further corrections or argument, and although I could never recall her taking more than a cursory glance at the *Border Morning Mail* herself, she obviously knew Mr Sukarno had more than mispronunciation of his name against him as far as my father was concerned. He was a 'commo' and one of those Asians who were all sitting huddled together north of us staring at Australia and just waiting to pounce on our wide open spaces. And, anyway, there was no indication that Dad had heard her, as he delivered the final word.

'You'd think they'd be a bit grateful wouldn't you? All we did for them during the war.'

Once a month during the summer, my mother would take a Sunday off from the café. That was the day we went to Dora Dora. Going there was an ideal outing for us all:

Mum, my brother Pete and I would spend the afternoon swimming and Dad would spend the afternoon drinking. So everyone was reasonably happy. Dora Dora was in fact just the name of the pub. The town itself—if you could call a pub, three houses, a small hall and a post office a town— was called Talmalmo and straddled a bend in the gravel road between Jingellic and Bowna. When it came to summer, Dora Dora had two great advantages.

The first was its location a few hundred yards from the Murray River, which, unlike the Ten Mile and the Billabong, didn't dry up in summer. Even though it meant a drive of thirty miles or so through forest country across the narrow, winding Tunnel Road, it was worth it. The second advantage it had was Alf Wright.

As far as publicans go, nobody came anywhere near Alf. Not for him the surly take-it-or-leave-it attitude of Flora McLennan or the casual off-handedness of Jack Quinlan. Here was a bloke who looked like Bud Abbott—short and chubby with dark, slicked-back hair and dark horn-rimmed glasses. Alf wore a permanent smile on his oval face as he told endless yarns and played practical jokes on any unsuspecting motorist who called in for a drink, much to the delight of the regulars.

A quick-change expert, one minute Alf was asking a visitor what he wanted to drink, then dropping out of sight behind the bar to re-emerge in a gorilla suit to hand over the beer. Other times he'd walk out the pub's front door and come back a few minutes later as a British army officer, all uniform, moustache and tin hat. People came from miles away to have a drink at the Dora Dora Pub because, thanks to Alf and his unique establishment, its fame had spread well beyond the banks of the Murray. Newspaper and magazine writers from the big cities carried stories about Alf and the trinkets and memorabilia he'd collected over the years.

The bar was only a small room at one end of the timber hotel and there wasn't a spare inch of space on its walls. They carried everything from oddly shaped beer bottles, World War II army colour patches, stuffed snakes and Murray cod pulled from the river just down the hill, spears, pistols, shotguns and muskets and even a joystick from a Japanese Zero fighter. Pride of place was a sign that announced FREE BEER TOMORROW which, according to Alf, just proved that tomorrow never came. Eventually, space became so limited that when his favourite calendar arrived every year he'd have to tack it to the ceiling. If any visitor asked for the date they were told to look up.

My father and Alf had become good friends over the years, and Dad admired Alf for what he was prepared to do for his customers. If you were ever on the river bank on a Saturday night it was not unusual to see Alf three or four times during the evening; due to drinking rules, Victorians (on the southern side of the river) had to cross the border to get a drink once the pubs there closed at six o'clock. This was the reason Alf kept a little row boat just up the river from where we would be swimming. As six o'clock came and went a set of car headlights could be seen approaching the river on the other side, until the car stopped at the bank and the driver sounded the horn. That would be the signal for Alf to appear at the front door of the pub, walk down through the paddock to the river, row across and bring the thirsty customers over to the New South Wales side, where they could drink on into the night. At the end of it all, he'd ferry them back in the darkness, a journey which must have been hazardous for him at times—you often heard loud laughter and the clink of bottles among his passengers as Alf groaned against the Murray's current.

Not that Alf's was the only hazardous journey undertaken of an evening. The Tunnel Road, which twisted its way through thick forests towards Holbrook and was the only way home from Dora Dora, was a steep, narrow stretch of gravel that had been built during the Great Depression to provide people with work.

Even in daylight, after a five- or six-hour drinking session it was not for the faint hearted. It must have been even worse for my mother, who couldn't drive but was terrified my father would go to sleep at the wheel. Whenever he looked like running off the road she would shout at him to stop the car. He'd then get out, walk to the front of the car and, in the glare of the headlights, run up the road and back again several times, which was his way of snapping awake when the effects of alcohol and tiredness started to combine. Sometimes this procedure would take place two or three times before the lights of Holbrook came into view.

Such was my father's inability to by-pass one of the 'essential' roadside hotels that running up and down the road in the glow of the taxi's headlights became part of his procedure at night. Much to my mother's concern, what the taxi had done was provide flexibility of movement, which filled the gap in my father's life created by the loss of easy access to McLennan's hotel. She couldn't help but notice that the 'essential' pubs had begun to play a large part in my father's working life as, no matter which direction he ventured on taxi assignments from Holbrook, the well-worn paths were marked by stopping points along the way.

While most of the work was local—around town for a shilling or two, or out to a shearing shed or homestead for a pound or two—it was the occasional longer jobs my father relished, journeys which were defined not solely by the value of the job itself but also by the pubs along the way. Thus, a taxi hire to Tarcutta to the north involved a call at Jack Quinlan's Billabong, and a hire to Culcairn a session at the Morven Hotel which conveniently split the eighteen-mile journey in half. But it was the forty-mile job between Holbrook and Albury, to collect a Holbrook passenger off the *Spirit of Progress* from Melbourne or to take a Holbrook punter to the Albury Races, which was the most attractive. McLennan's in Albury could then form the anchor point of a day-long excursion.

While my father's undertaking experiences gave him a healthy disregard for the Woomargama cemetery, his feelings for Lou Draper's Woomargama pub were quite the opposite and the nine-mile drive from Holbrook was just long enough to work up a thirst. Depending on whether he was on his own or with the agreement of his fare, after a session there it was south to the Mullengandra Hotel, a few miles further down the road. Of them all, and despite his long affection for McLennan's, it was Mullengandra's Royal Oak Hotel that was my father's favourite.

George Ross's Royal Oak was a low-line brick and cement structure flanked by two giant oak trees on the edge of the Hume Highway. In fact, the Royal Oak could be easily mistaken for part of the highway itself, its car park merely a gravel strip which stretched from the edge of the highway bitumen to the dark green bull-nosed verandah running the length of the building. Old George Ross was a big, jowly man with thinning dark hair, who always wore an open-necked shirt crossed by black braces that held up his dark blue trousers. As publicans go, George had not an ounce of the effusiveness of Dora Dora's Alf Wright. A taciturn fellow, when he talked it was more of a mumble, as if his mouth didn't want to be doing anything strenuous, but he was stuck with the problem of running a pub and that was all about serving beer and talking so George really had no option.

'G'day Mick,' was the traditional greeting when my father walked through the door, said in a tired, slightly disappointed tone, as it he'd expected my father a bit earlier but now he was here he might as well pull him a beer. George's son Bill, who was about my father's age, would occasionally appear from somewhere at the back of the hotel and offer to help serve in the bar. Not that his assistance was required all that often as it was rare to find more than three people drinking there at any one time; God knows where they came from as the only other building at Mullengandra was a church a few hundred yards further down the road. Bill was even less of a conversationalist than George which often made me wonder what my father found to talk about for the hours he spent there.

My father would then continue to Albury, and once there, time was always found for a round or two of drinks at McLennan's before setting out to repeat the process in reverse on the journey home. Most times, particularly if it was a job home from the Albury races, the passengers involved didn't object to a brief stopover at the Royal Oak, but in some ways it was a tribute to my father's persuasive powers that he never failed to make at least the stop at Mullengandra no matter who he was carrying at the time.

I once heard George Ross tell the story about one night when my father called in for a drink on his way home from Albury. After first downing a beer or two, he asked George to set up three seven-ounce glasses of raspberry and lemonade so he could take them to the car. When over the next half an hour several more such requests were made, George's curiosity got the better of him and he asked my father who was waiting in the car outside. It turned out to be three Catholic nuns from St Patrick's school at Holbrook who'd hired the taxi to take them home from a week-long religious retreat at their Albury parish.

George went out to the car to say a brief hullo before they drove off and said that the nuns had no complaints about their stopover. When he raised the subject the next time my father called in, he was told that the only difficult moment came when my father's bladder finally decided it had had enough while they were coming down the Woomargama Gap about seven miles short of Holbrook.

'Sisters, I'm sorry,' he'd said. We'll just have to stop for a moment.'

'That's all right Mr Eames,' replied one of the nuns. 'We know what it's like when nature calls.' They sat silently in the darkness while Dad slipped off quietly into the bushes behind.

Everyone in the bar laughed at the story. But I doubt my mother would have found it very funny—she could see this was part of a problem that was gradually worsening.

19

The dancing ducks

The end of the football season in 1951 coincided with the completion of my mother's first year as the proprietor of the Australian Café, and you could notice something different about her. Maybe it was because, for the first time in her life, she had ownership and responsibility for something which was almost totally without influence from my father. The fact that he showed absolutely no interest in the café's operation, particularly while he was occupied with his coaching commitments, meant that she alone had to oversee the outfitting of refrigerators and cooking facilities and the expensive decisions necessary to purchase them. Upon her, too, had fallen the tension-filled early months of watching and waiting to see whether her venture would succeed or fail, all the while committing herself to costly new orders during the regular visits of the Allens sweets van or the man from Four'nTwenty Pies and monitoring what was required in the kitchen and even how much malt and flavouring was needed for the milkshakes.

As the business had gradually built up over the twelve months so too had her self assurance and confidence. She had even reached the point where she no longer found it necessary to ask Dad's opinion on anything to do with the café, even when he was inclined to show interest. And, though it was completely foreign to her nature, she'd resorted to cutting Dad short when he levelled criticism at what she was doing.

Despite her early fears to the contrary and much to my mother's surprise, one of the main reasons for the early success of the Australian Café was due not to passing truck drivers or locals wanting late dinners but to what went on each Tuesday and Saturday night at the nearby shire hall.

While the summer months might have robbed the town of its main sporting preoccupation, the shire hall's year-round, twice-weekly movies provided continuous entertainment. And, as it would turn out, the early success or failure of Mum's café venture would have much to do with a short time frame of no more than twenty minutes every Tuesday and Saturday night. That was interval, when movie patrons streamed out of the hall to buy enough milkshakes, ice-creams, chocolates and musk sticks to see them through the second half. My mother's early concerns had been due to the fact that Jimmy Prineas' café was on the corner directly across the street from the shire hall; it was therefore the nearest replenishment point for those coming out at interval. Anyone wanting to buy something at Edna Eames' establishment would have to walk past

Prineas' to get there and, since they'd been in the habit of going to Prineas' for more years than anyone could remember, there was no guarantee their habits would change just because there was another similar outlet fifty yards further on.

But my mother hadn't figured on one thing. With limited time available, and with a queue four or five deep to reach Prineas' counter, the trickle of people on that first night who ventured further north, most probably curious to see what the Australian Café had to offer, soon became a mini flood. The result was that my mother soon had her own brief problem of a counter three deep with customers anxiously waving their ten-shilling notes and shouting orders so they wouldn't miss the start of the second show. Chaotic it may have been but it was a good problem to have and provided that early cash flow she needed to survive the first months.

My mother should not have been surprised, though, that it would be the shire hall which would help get her through the early period. If there was one thing that threatened Lieutenant Norman Holbrook's premier place in the town's history, it was the Holbrook shire hall.

It dominated not only in sheer size—its red brick and white cement façade peering down on the rest of the town from its prime position—but also in importance. Over the years pretty well everything of significance that had occurred in Holbrook took place at the shire hall. During World War II, when it had been better known as the

School of Arts, its elevated, deep-set stage was the venue for functions which resulted in Holbrook laying claim to the title of Australia's biggest donor towards wartime Liberty Loans. When they weren't busy raising money for such a cause the local womenfolk used the vast polished floorboards to pack Red Cross parcels and make camouflage nets.

Such activities proved so popular that the locals refused to let the end of the war dampen their enthusiasm. So they hosted a monthly event which became known as the Amateur Hour, and anyone who could sing, dance or play a musical instrument was in high demand. There were dances, too, which were non-stop affairs, and Andy Standfort on the saxophone, Frank Baldwin on drums and Mrs Gordon on the piano played until they dropped. Every now and again they'd talk Billy Bright, the local drover, into performing. But while Billy would burst into song at the drop of a middy in the bar at the Top Pub he was known to suffer the odd embarrassing case of stage fright when asked to perform sober in front of the crowd at Amateur Hour.

Occasionally there'd be a surprise appearance by Alf Wright's Dora Dora Blacks, a small group of locals from Talmalmo who'd managed to find enough charcoal and black paint to give their impression of a corroboree. Most times however, they largely succeeded in frightening many of the children in the audience. But the act the crowd most waited for was Micky Deep and his Dancing Ducks.

Mick's main role in life was running Deeps Transport service but when it came to entertainment he knew how to tantalise a crowd. His act always began with a slow, deliberate walk to a table set up on the stage, followed by the equally painstaking placement of a small raised platform, its lower half hidden from the crowd by a curved iron sheet. The expectant crowd would watch as Mick fiddled around beneath the back of the platform, then the two Deep ducks were ceremoniously placed on its flat surface. Since they started to dance almost immediately, Mick was careful to keep one hand on each of the birds in case they became too enthusiastic and jumped off the table. That never happened, however, and no matter how many times Mick and his ducks performed over the years it always brought the house down. (Mind you, it might have burnt the house down instead if the little Bunsen burner blazing under the ducks' platform had set the table alight!)

Over six feet tall and wafer thin, there was hardly anything Mick Deep wouldn't turn his hand to when it came to entertainment, even running the boxing tent each year at the Holbrook Show. Never one to deny the patrons their money's worth, if he couldn't encourage a local to take on the visiting pugilist, Mick wouldn't hesitate to hop into the ring himself.

The talent Mick most prided himself on was riding a pushbike backwards. After a long session at the pub one night, the local police sergeant spotted him weaving his way home and threatened to charge him with riding under the influence. In the ensuing discussion Mick argued that the ultimate test as to whether or not he was drunk would be to ride his bike backwards. Thinking this was a fair bet and unaware of Mick's hidden talents, the sergeant watched in awe as Mick cycled off backwards down the footpath. He was forced to let Mick off uncharged.

After that victory Mick added his backwards cycling skills to his Holbrook Show performance agenda and, every year, along with running the boxing, he'd challenge Karly Bounader, the picture show man, to a bicycle race over a set distance. Mick would ride his bike backwards while Karly rode the conventional way, but the fact that Karly weighed close to twenty-five stone (according to Mick's reckoning anyway) made it a fairly even contest. I don't know who won most of the races but I suspect, knowing the way showbiz works, they probably took it in turns to win.

20

The picture show man

Despite his massive size and dark Middle Eastern complexion, Karly Bounader was a gentle giant of a man who, with his brother Abe, a man of similar dimensions, had been in the country picture show business since early in the century. The Bounaders owned four theatres in all, but Karly had his hands full running Wodonga four or five nights a week and Holbrook every Tuesday and Saturday. And I doubt that any contribution he may have made to the early success of the Australian Café would have crossed Karly's mind.

He'd first started showing the movies at Holbrook years before, in a building further up the town's main street near the old post office site. That came to an end one night when he was halfway through a screening of Rudolf Valentino's *The Great Lover*, when a piece of fluff became caught on the film. He should have stopped the film rolling to extract the errant fluff but instead tried to remove it with a screwdriver—with the result that the film ignited and the building burnt down. After that the films were moved to the shire hall, its bigger screen, more seating and high ceiling providing a much improved venue.

Although his family came from Gundagai, seventy-five miles up the highway towards Sydney, Karly had been a long-term resident of Holbrook and those who could go back a bit said he'd been married twice. But neither union had brought him much happiness; the first one ended tragically after only two months when the horse pulling their sulky was spooked by a car and crashed, sending one of the sulky shafts through Karly's wife's chest. The second marriage didn't last long either—some of Karly's relatives thought she was 'a bit flighty'. Maybe, though, she wasn't looking forward to the living conditions Karly offered: a corrugated iron shed just up from St Patrick's Catholic school in the main street, furnished with not much more than a bed, a tap, an oversized handbasin to wash in and with an outside toilet.

But while his living conditions might have been sparse, Karly's imprint on the town was just the opposite and in many ways he was as much a feature as the old shire hall itself.

My memory of Karly is an image of a man of vast bulk riding a bicycle with the handlebars reversed back-to-front, weaving around the streets balancing an assortment of paraphernalia around his person. Dangling from the handlebars would be a metal bucket containing paste, a mix of flour, water and alum—or clag as Karly called it—to be used for pasting his bill posters on galvanised billboards strategically placed on fences around the town. These would announce to passers-by the coming attractions for the next two weeks. He also had a smaller, clagless version which would be placed in the front window of places like the Australian Café. Somehow, across one shoulder, he could manage to balance the huge calico brush used to daub the paste, while on the other shoulder hung the small stepladder he used to reach the required height up the fence. No one ever saw him come to grief despite the awkwardness of the arrangement on the bike, and as a kid the most exciting part was watching him keep the whole lot together while he brought the bike to a stop alongside a target fence.

As for the rest of the procedure for bringing us the movies every Tuesday and Saturday night, getting it all together was sometimes easier said than done. Part of the reason for this was the logistics. First, the films had to come by train from Melbourne or Sydney to Albury, where they would be collected by Karly's old cycling opponent Micky Deep for the journey to Holbrook. The necessity to cover so much overland territory meant that occasionally things went wrong, a problem compounded if a particular film was larger than normal. The film for the four-hour long *Ten Commandments*, for instance, would be spread over not one but four or five reels. One only had to go astray en route and you might have missed out on a commandment or two!

Once, several containers did fall off the truck near Table Top. Mick retrieved them okay but he must have mixed up the order of the containers. The result was that Karly had to scramble to splice the right pieces together again minutes before the last half of the movie was due to be shown.

Nor did it help that the projectors in all the Bounader theatres had differing spool sizes which meant Karly had to individually prepare every inch of film before the opening credits rolled. No wonder he had a tendency to select the soothing tones of Richard Tauber or Caruso for the half-time music, as not knowing what technical problem lurked in front of him during the next session must have added to his anxiety.

Most times everything worked out, although sometimes when it didn't it had its lighter moments. Like the Saturday night we were watching a World War II drama about a German submarine crew attacking a North Sea convoy. The British destroyer had located the U-boat and just as the submarine came to rest silently on the ocean floor, the sweat-covered faces of the terrified crew looking upwards as they waited for the next depth charge to explode, the screen suddenly went black. After a few moments, as the customary foot stomping started to echo from the polished floorboards, Karly came out of the projection box to announce the film had broken and he couldn't repair it that night. The sub's crew, everyone agreed, would just have to stay under water until the following Tuesday.

Still, for sixpence admission and an extra sixpence to go upstairs we got our money's worth. That's why, when Karly died, we knew things at the shire hall wouldn't be quite the same anymore.

21

The long-distance undertaker

Karly Bounader suffered a heart attack and died beside his bed in the corrugated tin shed he called home. It was some time before his brother Abe found him and started to make arrangements for the funeral.

It didn't take long for the probable complications of this particular funeral to dawn on my father, and when Abe told him the family wanted Karly buried seventy-five miles away in Gundagai he realised immediately that this was going to be no ordinary burial.

Most of his concern was created by the fact that the only experience he'd had so far with long-distance undertaking had been two burials at Woomargama and, what with one involving a coffin that wouldn't fit and the other a snake in the grave, neither of them was listed among his favourite memories.

Then there was the Essex. The old girl might have looked elegant but when it came to venturing seventy-five miles up the Hume Highway, looking elegant was about all you could say on her behalf. My father considered that the days of taking a vehicle as old as the Essex such a distance had long since passed and anyway, with her wooden-spoked wheels, primitive suspension and underpowered engine, she was anything but comfortable or easy to drive. But in this case there wasn't much option so he set about organising the logistics.

The first thing to do, thanks to bitter experience, was to charge the Essex's battery, but he realised he'd also need some help with this funeral. Nace Kane volunteered to give him a hand though they agreed that at least four people would be needed simply to manhandle Karly's giant frame into the casket and whenever the casket needed to be manhandled after that.

Since neither liked the idea of advertising they had a dead body in the back of the hearse as they drove along the Hume Highway, they decided to use the storage space hidden under the normal area for carrying the coffin. At least then it would be out of sight and a little discreet.

Kelly O'Brien was out fencing on the Sydney Road when my father found him and explained the difficulties they might confront with timing and manpower. But, as it turned out, Kelly helped solve the manpower problem. He knew that the grave at Gundagai would have to be dug the morning of the funeral and, having done some fencing in the Gundagai district in the past, he also knew something about the risk of striking hard gravel at the Gundagai cemetery. So to make sure he didn't have to dig alone, he rang Gordon McLaurin.

'Karly Bounader's dead,' said Kelly.

'I already know that,' replied Gordon, having heard the previous day.

'I'll need a hand, mate,' said Kelly, 'They want to bury him in Gundagai and I might need some help to get the grave down.'

Such a request was not unusual from Kelly, who would call on Gordon's help when faced with a gravedigging job at short notice on the basis that two shovels were quicker than one.

But Gordon thought he could detect a hint of alcohol in Kelly's voice and suspected the need might not be all that urgent. 'Sorry Kelly, I'm flat out here on the property,' he replied.

'I can't handle it on my own,' said Kelly, with pleading in his voice, explaining some of the difficulties he might face.

By now Gordon could tell the request was genuine and agreed to help. Just as he was about to hang up, Kelly added, 'And bring along some gelli. I've been there before and we might need it.' Neither was that an unusual request from his gravedigger mate.

Gordon's property, Dalriada, had an old gold mine on it so he knew how to handle explosives. And although it was illegal to use such assistance when it came to digging graves it had nevertheless come in handy in the past when Kelly had struck the odd seam of rock or gravel.

That settled, Kelly told Gordon they'd pick him up early the next day.

It was already a warm April morning by the time Gordon, waiting near the cattle ramp which separated Dalriada's entrance from the highway, spotted the black hearse chugging towards him in the distance. It passed through his mind that they might be asking quite a lot of the old girl, what with twenty-five stone of Karly in the back, the bulk of Nace Kane in the front with my father, and himself and Kelly in the cramped rear seat. But as they moved off and my father ground slowly through the gears, the Essex seemed to be handling it okay.

By the strained look on my father's face, however, Gordon could tell that there was some uncertainty about what lay ahead of them since this early stage along the flat, open country past the Mangoplah turnoff and Little Billabong was the easy part. Gordon knew my father would be only too aware that, before they reached Tarcutta, the first major town, they would have to cross the Kyeamba Gap, although once through there it was pretty flat for the rest of the way. Gaps, or particular hills, were a feature of he roads around Holbrook—elevated points which the locals used to identify certain areas en route to other townships. For instance, Blue Metal Hill, a long downhill slope of distinguishable blue bitumen surface, marked around the halfway point between Woomargama and Mullengandra. In the same way, the Woomargama Gap was the only prominent climb on the road between Holbrook and Woomargama, and the Wantigong Gap straddled the road between Holbrook and Jingellic.

The Kyeamba Gap wasn't much of a gap, just a fairly steady climb up several hundred feet to reach a section where the high sides of the original road cutaway reared up a few extra yards on either side of the highway. Hardly, therefore, a gap to speak of, but for some reason that was what everyone called it.

Later, Gordon would be glad he had kept his thoughts to himself because, almost from the moment the road surface started to climb towards Kyeamba, the Essex's engine began to give Dad trouble. First there was an occasional miss, just a momentary loss of power before the engine took up again. This was followed a few minutes later by a more pronounced hiccup or two and Gordon noticed my father fiddling repeatedly with the short, steel fuel-mixture lever on the inside of the wooden steering wheel. This seemed to work for a mile or so but as soon as the gap climb started in earnest the engine misfiring returned, gradually worsening until the whole vehicle started to shudder and the engine cut out completely. By this time the country undertaker was already pointing the wheels towards the side of the road.

'The bloody thing's vaporising,' announced my father, as they all piled out onto the verge. 'We'll have to wait until it cools down.'

They all knew what vaporising was—a fault in the fuel pump combined with the hot weather, causing the petrol to evaporate as it passed through the pump. All except Kelly, that is, who hardly knew a fuel pump from a fan belt, and hated motorised transport with a passion.

Faced with what was turning out to be even less time to dig the grave, he couldn't help himself. 'Bastard of a thing,' Gordon heard Kelly swear, directing his words at the open bonnet of the hearse. 'If it's a bloody horse at least you can sell it or shoot it,' he continued, providing a bushman's view of the situation.

There are few remedies for a vaporising fuel pump out on the road but my father would have known that all was not lost. The secret was to firstly give it enough time to cool down and then once on the road again gradually get up enough speed to throw the gear level into neutral. Once that happened and the car coasted silently the engine would idle, thus keeping the pump's workload down and everything under the bonnet at a much lower tempera-ture. After a short distance coasting, you could slip the car back into gear and gradually build up speed again to repeat the process. It wasn't the most ideal way to travel long distances but at least you could get there. The trouble they currently faced, though, was they were on an uphill slope and the only coasting they could do was backwards. Once over the top, however, my father was confident they could make it.

So they got out and impatiently waited the fifteen minutes or so that my father said they'd need for the fuel pump to return to normal. And, sure enough, the Essex burst into life at the first attempt. Relieved, they all piled in again and the Essex resumed the climb. But their relief was short lived and a few hundred yards further on up the hill she stopped again.

Out they tumbled, prepared for another wait. On this occasion however, they were just about to climb back aboard when Nace Kane stopped them. 'I think we should see how Karly is going,' he suggested.

They'd forgotten all about Karly—not that there was much he could do to help, of course, but Gordon felt a pang of conscience nonetheless. After all, he'd been dead a few days and the coffin had spent the last hour or so in the warm confines of the hearse's hidden rear compartment.

Gordon McLaurin would never forget the contrast between Nace Kane's cultured tones and what followed. Parked facing upwards on the slope, the Essex was at an angle which would normally be of great benefit to anyone wishing to use minimum effort to slide a coffin out the back. You can imagine their surprise when the moment the two little black doors at the back were swung open out came Karly and the coffin—separately.

You don't have to be Albert Einstein to work out what had happened. There was only one size of coffin in my father's inventory and Karly, due to his large size, had only just made it into that. Now, after several days there and subjected in the last hour or so to steadily warmer conditions in the rear of the hearse, expanding forces had simply proved too much and the casket had burst open around him.

They all stood there dumbfounded for a moment, staring down at Karly and the split coffin lying on the road verge between them. Again it was Nace Kane who broke the silence, although this time his cultured tones had a high-pitched ring of panic about them.

'What'll we do?' he said. Then again, 'What'll we do? How will we ever get him back?'

Despite the fact that he'd repeated himself, Nace wasn't looking forward to any answer he might get. Gordon wasn't saying anything at all, still struggling to get over the shock of it all. The next words, probably predictably, came from Kelly O'Brien, and if they were designed to add further shock they succeeded admirably.

'We'll gut 'im,' he exclaimed.

Not wanting to know whether Kelly was serious, neither Nace nor my father said much after that and, as if acting on some hidden signal, both walked slowly away until they disappeared behind a tall gum tree on the edge of the bush. There they stayed and every now and then Gordon would look up to catch one of them peering out from behind the tree. Once or twice, when Nace looked out he asked in a voice now fraught with concern, 'How are you going there?'

'We'll soon be right,' came the reassuring response.

What Kelly and Gordon did that day neither would ever say, not even years later when the Kyeamba Gap incident had become Holbrook folklore. To be sure, neither Nace Kane nor my father wanted to know anyway. They both came out from behind the tree in time to help the two bushmen twist a length of eight-gauge wire Kelly had cut from a nearby fence around the sides of the coffin to bind it together again.

The extended delay, however, had had a beneficial effect on the Essex's fuel pump. She started first turn and delighted her passengers by making it over the gap without incident to the welcome flat country on the other side.

Their troubles weren't over, however, as by the time they reached the cemetery there was barely an hour and a half left for the grave to be dug. On top of that, Kelly wasn't more than five feet down when, as he'd predicted, he struck gravel.

Out of the corner of his eye Gordon could see the first of the mourners starting to turn onto the approach road a few hundred yards west of the cemetery when he heard Kelly say in a whisper, 'Go and get me some of that "material" of yours.' Since neither Nace nor my father were aware of the gelignite Kelly figured what they didn't know wouldn't hurt them.

But Nace Kane did hear him and, his suspicions aroused, he asked, 'What are you going to do, Kelly?'

'I'm going to stick a charge down there,' replied Kelly, unashamedly.

'You can't do that. They'll hear it miles away,' said Nace, indignant at the crudity of such a gravedigging process.

Gordon figured, however, that the dramas of the Kyeamba Gap had already taken their toll on Nace and he was probably wondering why he'd agreed to come along in the first place. He thought he'd better say something just to calm things down.

'It's too late for the gelli anyway, Kelly,' said Gordon, motioning towards the bottom of the cemetery road where an increasing throng of mourners was already heading in their direction. 'Why don't we just ask them to wait while we finish the job,' he offered.

'Bugger that,' retorted Kelly, by now deciding he was losing both the argument and any desire he had to dig the grave any deeper. With that he picked up the shovel and turned his back on all of them, setting off for the seclusion of the cemetery perimeter and tossing over his shoulder as he went. 'Doesn't matter anyway. He won't jump out.'

Late that afternoon, the funeral behind them, they bought two bottles of red wine at the Gundagai Hotel to sustain them on the way home. No one said much during the journey but at least the Essex, probably helped now by the cooler evening temperatures, gave them no trouble.

By the time they reached Holbrook's northern outskirts the wine was gone and Kelly suggested they should stop for a beer at the Top Pub. Not getting much enthusiasm from the front seat he asked again.

'C'mon Nace let's have a drink.'

'Absolutely not,' came the reply, the cultured tones once again in evidence. 'I'm going straight home and having a bloody good shower. The end of a ghastly day.'

'That's for me too,' said the country undertaker.

It was the only time Gordon had ever heard my father knock back the offer of a beer.

The incident at the Kyeamba Gap, much more of a disaster than flat batteries and lack of either speed or comfort, probably did more than anything else to seal the fate of the

Essex. It had confirmed in my father's mind that, when it came to covering any distance greater than the nine miles to Woomargama, she was just not up to the task.

So he began to look around for a replacement and, in the meantime, devised some other method to overcome the distance problem. The Bounader funeral had been something of a rare occurrence, however, in that a Holbrook undertaker had come from out of town to bury a resident of another country town the size of Gundagai, a role that usually fell to the town's own resident funeral director.

There was, nonetheless, still a requirement to be able to carry out a more common chore—the positioning or body transfer. This was necessary when a death occurred in the Holbrook area but the burial was to take place elsewhere, something which often happened as a result of a fatal car accident on the Hume Highway. On such occasions, because of the distances involved, two undertakers at opposite ends would generally agree on a halfway point at which they would execute the transfer, thus cutting down the travelling for each of them. Albury was one of the simpler towns to coordinate this with, as Dad's old friend Bill Lester was happy to meet at a rendezvous around halfway between the two and, much to my father's delight, that particular rendezvous point turned out to be somewhere around George Ross's Mullengandra Hotel.

As it would turn out though, longer distances were to remain a problem for my father. But initially, when the new hearse arrived, he felt his problems might be solved.

It certainly looked that way at first, as the 1938 8/90 Buick was a quantum leap up from the Essex. By the time the panel beaters at Kane's Motors had installed the side windows and ducoed her grey with black trim, the ex-NSW ambulance appeared to be a country undertaker's dream come true. The 8/90 stood high off the ground with a driving compartment which still retained the sweet smell of leather and the polished finish of a pre-war American supercar. And, unlike the refined, timid old Essex, a remnant from another era, she had power to burn. The long, curvaceous bonnet concealed an eight-cylinder engine which would have ideally suited the speed requirements of its role as an ambulance, but my father was soon to find out that this speed performance characteristic brought with it several significant drawbacks.

One was her weight. The original conversion from a Buick sedan to an ambulance had increased considerably the rear-end weight of the vehicle with little compensatory suspension, steering or braking improvements and, given my father's impatience when confronted with poor driving by others on the road, it didn't take him long to discover these shortcomings first-hand.

Within a week or two of her arrival the Buick was to undergo her first test. We were returning along the highway from a body transfer at Tarcutta when a blue and white Ford Zephyr overtook the Buick and committed (according to my father's standards anyway) one of driving's most inexcusable offences: cutting sharply across the Buick's bows, causing my father to momentarily check the car.

Immediately, his whole body seemed to tense and, despite the fact we were already travelling at around fifty miles an hour, there was a surge of power as my father stomped on the accelerator and the Buick set off after the Zephyr.

This, of course, was not a new experience for anyone riding in a car with my father at the wheel. No words were ever spoken, no explanations necessary but the look on his face left you in no doubt that here was a lesson about to be learned by the offending motorist.

Within a mile or so, with the horsepower difference well and truly in favour of the big eight-cylinder, the Buick had drawn alongside the Zephyr. This was the point at which, under his normal procedure on such occasions and provided the road ahead was clear, Dad would 'hang' alongside the offender for several hundred yards, all the while fixing the other driver with a glare which, if translated into words would say something like 'Okay, smartarse, don't ever do that to anyone again,' after which there would be a further kick on the accelerator and he would leave the motorist, now suitably chastened, in his wake.

That's the way it had always happened with the A70 Austin, anyway. On this occasion, I could see a brief look of astonishment on the other driver's face as he suddenly realised he'd been overtaken by a hearse, then we were accelerating away in front of him. But not for long.

By now we were travelling at well over eighty miles an hour and the effect of the hearse's massive rear bulk was starting to have all sorts of strange effects on the Buick. First of all she began to develop a swaying motion which gradually became more pronounced as my father tried to guide her back onto the left side of the road. This quickly grew worse as it began to have an impact on the front of the car, which appeared to want to float, until the steering became so light and ineffective that my father was forced to quickly reduce speed and restore stability before all three of us—Dad, me and the Buick—faced the prospect of leaving the highway at some speed.

Visibly shaken, my father was now forced to suffer the embarrassment of seeing the Zephyr flash past us, its driver wearing a wry smile on his face, doubtless having enjoyed the spectacle from behind. From that day forward there would be no further high speed pursuits with the Buick.

And then there was the petrol consumption. Compared to the Essex, the Buick was a thirsty beast, its weight and engine capacity dictating a fuel usage more akin to gallons to the mile than miles to the gallon, with the result that her use for even the shortest body transfer would be unnecessarily expensive. My father must have recalled Bill Lester's early advice never to use a hearse for anything beyond the journey to the local cemetery because he quickly got the idea of using Charlie Craig's ute for long-distance jobs.

When he wasn't kicking goals for Holbrook's premiership football team, Charlie Craig was a builder with an FJ Holden ute. Since the transfer of bodies could often be arranged at night it turned out to be relatively easy for my father and Charlie to come to an arrangement about using the white FJ.

While it wasn't mentioned at the time, my father was only too aware that one of the advantages of the FJ was it looked like any other vehicle that might be parked outside an en route pub when he stopped for a drink—thus avoiding having something as ostentatious as a hearse in full view in the hotel's car park. In fact, the FJ ute proved its value in this respect with my father's first transfer job, when he stopped for a drink at the Newmarket Hotel after collecting a customer from Albury.

The Newmarket was in East Albury and required a few minutes' diversion from the main Albury to Holbrook road. It was my uncle Dave's local watering hole, however, and therefore an occasional stop on the way home from Albury taxi assignments was required.

According to Uncle Dave's account, he and my father had been drinking with some others for an hour or so when my father announced he'd better head back to the ute and 'get the customer home'. No one believed him, of course and, confident it was just another undertaker joke which he tended to tell from time to time, bets were taken on whether or not he was telling the truth. Everyone in the bar, including those not part of Uncle Dave's group, was then invited outside to witness the unveiling as the FJ's black canvas cover was drawn back and the coffin exposed. Uncle Dave, who'd been an SP bookie all his life, said it was the easiest money he'd ever earned.

Though Charlie's ute may have provided a certain degree of discretion as well as economical advantages, it wasn't a complete answer to the problem of body transfers, the main disadvantage being limited space in the back. Sure, the black tonneau adequately covered the coffin from above, but no matter how you arranged it a normal-sized casket would still protrude a few inches or so out the back of the ute. This would prevent you from shutting the tailboard, which meant that anyone travelling behind had an unobstructed view of the rear end of a coffin.

My father's answer was to cover the rear end of the casket with an old grey army blanket, held against the coffin by a rope stretching across the back of the ute to stop the coffin sliding out. As usual it was another one of his shortcuts which was to prove only a temporary fix and one destined to come very close to disaster the night of the Euroa transfer.

The Euroa transfer involved a Victorian man who'd been fatally injured in a head-on crash on the highway north of Holbrook, and agreement had been reached for my father to meet the Melbourne undertaker at Euroa, 130 or so miles south of Holbrook.

It was mid afternoon before Charlie could release the ute. So by the time we had loaded the coffin, wrapped the blanket, fastened the rear rope and made the obligatory stop for Dad's few drinks at the Mullengandra Hotel, it was just on dusk as we approached Wangaratta, about fifty-five miles from our destination.

With the later-than-planned departure and the Mullen-gandra stop I could tell by the speed we were travelling that my father was hurrying things along to make our Euroa rendezvous point on time. Wangaratta is the biggest town between Albury and Euroa, and at that time the approach by road from the north took you along a section of the highway which crossed low, swampy river-flat country which often flooded when the Ovens River broke its banks in the rainy season. For this reason, this stretch of the highway featured a succession of narrow, short, humped bridges each of which rose slightly above the level of the road itself. There was a bunch of cars behind us as we approached the first of the bridges. My father had traversed this section of road hundreds of times before and knew the result if you went too fast, but on this occasion his mind must have been elsewhere, or perhaps concentrating on making up time. Whatever the reason, by the time we reached the first humped bridge he had done nothing to wash off the FJ's speed— with the result that the ute hit the first bridge so fast that the whole vehicle became airborne.

Suddenly there was complete silence as the wheels momentarily parted company with the road, followed by a bone-jarring thud as they returned, then several more seconds' delay before the casket in the back, rope stretched to the maximum, grey blanket now trailing in the slipstream, rejoined the utility with a resounding crash. For what seemed an eternity, neither of us dared to look back, fearful of a vision of fragmented wood and the casket's former contents strewn across the highway in front of a line of stalled traffic and stunned motorists.

Fortunately though, the rope had held and the only damage had been to one of the hinges on the tailboard which had buckled under the impact of the coffin.

It was the second time my father learned that vehicles carrying dead people are not necessarily designed for speed.

22

Death can be funny
at times

Most people attending a funeral probably don't take much notice of the undertaker. With the casket as the centre of attention, he's something of a peripheral being, sliding quietly here and there in an overseer's role, in the middle of things perhaps but not all that conspicuous.

In my father's case, had anyone noticed, they'd have seen a small man in a black, pin-striped suit, his dark hair combed sharply back above a face wearing a serious expression as would befit such an occasion. Apart from those occasions when the coffin didn't fit or a brown snake needed to be dispatched he was a picture of reflective solemnity, totally immersed in the seriousness of the business at hand.

But anyone who knew him would have realised that such an impression was a misleading one, and while I occasionally saw him wince when he entered a room and someone made the old crack about 'here comes the undertaker with a tape measure in his pocket to size us up', he appeared at times to find it easy to recognise that death can have its funny side.

Perhaps it was because it really didn't take much to bring out the humour which lay just below the surface in the undertaker's trade. For my father, maybe his quick identification of the funny side had much to do with where he came from—that blokey world of football friendships and the motor spare-parts business, both male dominated areas where humour and taking the mickey out of someone else's circumstances were just part of the camaraderie.

Looking back later, I would wonder whether the extrovert in him needed humour to act as a relief valve to help him deal with the at-times grim and immediate aftermath of a violent death, particularly when it involved people he knew. Whatever the reason, there was little doubt that humour was quick to surface whenever more than two undertakers gathered in the one place.

For most undertakers, including my father, humour fell into two categories. The first was that which was played out amongst family and friends, like taking bets on whether or not there was a body in the back of Charlie Craig's ute outside the Newmarket Hotel.

The second, and more significant, category was the one undertakers kept between themselves, which covered the more unusual and even bizarre. And while I don't think there were such things as undertakers' conventions in those days, had they been inclined to hold them, they could have sold tickets for the laughs.

Rarely, however, was a story ever told with the intention of showing disrespect for the dead. Rather, stories tended to evolve from circumstances surrounding a death or an incident at a funeral which brought out the best, or worst, in human nature.

Occasionally, as in the Newmarket Hotel case, such a story had its origins in a wager or a debt. This also occurred when one day my father and Sausage Jamison went to collect the body of a man who lived in a converted garage beside a two-storey block of flats.

It was already dark when they arrived and, not wishing to draw too much attention to their mission, my father decided to park the hearse down at the very end of the dead-end street, out of sight of the neighbours. In this case they'd bring the body out to it, rather than reverse the hearse up the laneway.

They'd quietly gone about their job in the garage, and were halfway down the driveway between the block of flats and the garage when my father heard a window in the upstairs flat slide open. A man's voice broke the silence, obviously directing his comments to someone else inside the flat: 'Bloody good thing. Now I won't have to pay that bastard the ten quid I owe him.' With that the window was slammed shut again and silence returned as my father and Sausage continued down the driveway.

Sometimes the stories came from other undertakers—one, strangely enough, involving an Essex similar to Dad's own which was operated by Ivan Lyons up at Tumbarumba.

Ivan and his Essex were within a hundred yards from the cemetery when the old Essex decided it had had enough and stopped dead. Fortunately for Ivan his own brand new mourning car was travelling immediately behind the hearse in the procession, so Ivan and its driver quickly swapped places. Ivan drove the new vehicle up behind the hearse and began to give the Essex a shove from behind to cover the remaining few yards to the cemetery gate. He'd only pushed a short distance when out of the corner of his eye he saw the deceased man's daughter walking towards him. Fearing the worst he waited for what was to come but he needn't have worried.

'No problem Ivan,' she said with a smile. He didn't want to go there anyway.'

At the end of the day, though, most of the stories about the lighter side of the business would have come from Albury, probably because, being a bigger town than Holbrook (or Tumbarumba for that matter), more people died there.

Alan Henshaw was an old friend of my father's. Along with Mike Egan, he had spent years working with Lester and Son and, like my father, also had a 'money' story. It was about the day he and Mike were burying a fellow at Albury cemetery, when one of the mourners stepped forward and tossed a handful of coins and several notes into the grave, announcing in a loud voice as the silver clattered onto the coffin, 'There you are, you old bugger. Now don't say I never bought you a drink.' That said, he stepped back again and stood silent, his head bowed.

Alan could also attest that domestic grievances could bubble to the surface at the most inopportune times. One of the most memorable occurred the afternoon they were burying a man in a section of the Albury cemetery off Union Road. It was a big funeral, with several hundred in attendance. The service had barely drawn to a close, with the widow and close family of the deceased still standing at the grave, when a tall, red-headed woman walked out of the crowd until she was alongside the grieving party. She looked directly at the sobbing widow and announced at the top of her voice, 'What are you crying for, you bitch? He was *my* husband and you stole him from me.' Then, turning towards the shocked crowd, she added, 'Did you all know that?' Alan said he hadn't the faintest idea whether the crowd knew it or not—but what they certainly didn't know was where to look!

On occasions Alan and Mike would have to visit the Albury Base Hospital to collect a body and would try to make their 'collections' at night, out of sensitivity towards the other patients. Once, they'd made several visits in a short space of time, and Alan began to notice an elderly man always sitting in the same chair in a room at one end of a corridor. No matter what time they passed, he was always there, sitting silently in the chair.

Finally, when Mike asked the ward nurse about him she explained that he was almost one hundred years old and insisted on spending all his time in the chair, even nodding off in it when he couldn't keep his eyes open any longer. That seemed to satisfy Mike, who turned to Alan as they walked away and said, 'If I was almost a hundred I wouldn't want to close my eyes either.'

When it came to handling the death of a close one, people's faith could be called into question—although that might have been only part of the explanation for what happened on one occasion in Albury.

According to Alan, the deceased woman had been in a de facto relationship with a fellow who had fallen victim to the booze. He'd had a mate who had found himself in a similar situation. The woman appeared to have no other relatives or friends except for these two.

It had been agreed that the funeral would take place at 1 p.m. When the morning of the funeral arrived, however, the poor fellow had trouble remembering the timing involved, a situation which became increasingly apparent to Mike and Alan when he turned up at the funeral director's offices at 9 a.m. and then again at 10 a.m., both times to be told, 'No, the funeral's at 1 p.m.' Undeterred, he nonetheless turned up again at 11 a.m. and again at noon, each time a little more the worse for wear and each time to be told once again the correct time for the funeral.

When 12.45 p.m. came, however, and he was about to leave for the cemetery, Mike was dismayed to find the fellow was nowhere to be seen. Acting on a hunch he slipped a block or two down the street to find the pair propping up the bar at Ryan's Hotel. Mike bundled the two of them into his car and they headed for the cemetery.

As Mike expected, there was no one else at the cemetery when they arrived apart from Alan Henshaw and the

Baptist reverend, who by this time was anxious to get things under way. Everything went as normal until the reverend reached that part of the service where he invokes the religious interpretation of the life/death cycle with the words: 'The good Lord giveth and the good Lord taketh away.' At that, the chief mourner, who up till now had struggled to keep up with what was happening, suddenly broke his silence, stopping the reverend in his tracks.

'The good Lord must be a proper bastard,' he said, 'to take away a good woman like that.'

More silence followed while the reverend, still taken aback, asked Mike to fetch him a glass of water to help him regain his composure.

It was not always humans who filled the central roles in Mike and Alan's stories; in fact, the one they would both dine out on involved not a human reaction to death but that of an animal, in this case a prize cow.

The funeral was in a Murray River town not far from Albury and the deceased woman had been a top breeder of Murray Grey cattle, one of which, her champion cow, had won first prize at the Royal Melbourne Show. Such was the woman's regard for the animal that before she passed away she had decreed the cow should be the chief mourner at her funeral.

When the day of the funeral arrived the cow was brought to the church service in a horse float and cere-moniously unloaded. It stood solemnly while the casket was brought out and placed into the hearse. The cow was then loaded back into the horse float, which followed the hearse to the cemetery where the cow was unloaded again and, led by the deceased's granddaughter, it walked immediately behind the coffin to the gravesite. As the service concluded and just as Alan and Mike started to lower the coffin into the grave, the cow—which had been a silent witness to this point—suddenly mooed loudly in farewell. Alan and Mike were both there and they both swear it happened.

My father would not be outdone when it came to a good animal story, although his version was not quite so ceremonial—or legal. When it comes to pets there's a law against burying them with their owners, but I guess there is always going to be the odd one that slips through the net.

I noticed whenever he told this particular story my father would never name the town or, for that matter, tell it in front of my mother. At first I attributed the latter to his sensitivity, given that the lady who'd died had been a friend of my mother from her school days, and although they hadn't seen each other for years he'd offered to drive my mother to the funeral in western Victoria.

As it turned out the son of the deceased was also an undertaker. So I guess my father would have been looking forward to comparing notes, so to speak, when he arrived at the son's house where the body was available for viewing in the bedroom. The main object of attention for those sitting in the lounge room, however, turned out to be the deceased's elderly, wire-haired terrier; it seemed to have a problem, where it walked a few paces then its legs collapsed and it fell over. There'd then be a pause in the conversation while everyone watched the animal painfully drag itself back upright, only to stagger a few more paces before its back legs would once again give way.

After some minutes watching the old terrier repeat this performance as it wandered between the lounge room and the kitchen, my father heard someone in the group mutter, 'Look at the poor dog. It's missing her so much. Look what effect it's having on the thing.'

While my father could appreciate such a comment under the circumstances (as the dog had been the widowed lady's inseparable companion for almost twenty years) it was also fairly obvious to him that the dog had been this way long before the lady had died. Not wishing to shatter any illusions, however, and becoming a little tired of it all, he decided to walk out onto the verandah for a cigarette. Unfortunately the dog decided to follow and proceeded to repeat the sequence outside.

By the time my father had returned to the lounge room he noticed the animal's plight was still the main topic of discussion. But the conversation had moved on somewhat, to the point where the deceased's son announced, quite solemnly, 'Well, maybe we ought to put the dog down if it's that bad. It'll probably never get over it.'

There followed a short huddle and muted discussion in the kitchen between my father, the son and several of the relatives, after which the dog was not seen again. The son was, however, heard to comment his mother would be 'very happy under the circumstances' adding that 'everything will be completed with dignity'.

And so it was, with a respectful funeral service and a smooth cremation.

My parents were halfway home to Albury when my father foolishly made some light-hearted comment about the day's events being the first time he'd seen 'two for the price of one', at which there was a gasp from my mother as she realised for the first time what had taken place.

When my father looked across he saw the horrified expression on my mother's face as she exclaimed, 'My goodness. When they spread her ashes how will they know which are hers and which are the dog's?'

As my father told it, he let the question hang there. It was one he couldn't answer anyway.

23

A complex character

It was during the Holbrook years, as the mini empire of the Eames family took my father from spare parts man to taxi proprietor to country undertaker, with my mother's café excursion in between, that my father was to come into focus as a more complex, complicated character than he appeared on the outside. He'd managed to lift himself out of a behind-the-counter existence into a taxi business and the unlikely role of an undertaker—but through it all demonstrating, mainly due to drinking and gambling, that he was prepared to let opportunities slip through his fingers. Then, out of the blue, he'd start to toss around the idea of some new venture, often to the consternation of those around him.

His best mate Jock Hulme came close to getting it right when they were sitting in the café kitchen drinking beer one day, while my mother busied herself preparing savoury mince and vegetables for a customer at a table inside. My father had started to talk about establishing a spare parts shop in Holbrook to cater for the range of non-General Motors vehicles outside the orbit of Kane's Motors. As an old friend and part of the Nace Kane/Jim Woolley group who gambled with Dad at the RSL club, Jock would have known that not much of the money from the taxi fares was making it to the blue tin under the bed.

When they weren't playing cards there were the more convenient poker machines. Even if there wasn't a gambling resource in sight, Jock could count on my father pulling a ten-shilling note from his pocket and challenging him to a game of Riki Tiki, which involved each player producing a similar note and comparing the numbers on them. Apparently, whoever held the note with the most duplication of one number on it won the game and the notes themselves.

So when my father voiced his thoughts about adding a spare parts component to his business interests, Jock could see the pointlessness of it all. He cut in, half jokingly, 'Jesus Mick, you already feed 'em, drive 'em home and bury 'em. Why don't you let someone else look after their cars?'

Whether he realised it or not, Jock had tapped into the contradictions in my father. On one hand, here he was contemplating the launch of a new career, albeit one which he would have been completely comfortable with due to his background. On the other hand, he had still to prove his application to the business side of the ventures he already had on his plate. While he seemed eminently capable of recognising and seizing an opportunity and, initially at least, dedicating himself to making it a success—

whether it be coaching a football team, driving a cab or burying people—it was only a matter of time before my father would fall prey to the temptations presented by gambling or drink.

Perhaps the signs of such contradictions had always been there, even in his early working life. As a spare parts man he had few peers, and while even in those days the more glamorous side belonged to the car salesmen, a good spare parts man followed close behind in the pecking order. My father's secret seemed to be that he had been blessed with an incredible memory for numbers. All car spare parts were, at that time, identified by a six-figure number, no matter what the make or model, and such numbers were the critical currency of the spare parts man. Thus, when a customer arrived at the counter to request a set of big-end bearings for anything from a 1934 Chevrolet to a 1941 Dodge, most spare parts men had to leaf through a four-inch thick manual to identify the part and the appropriate number. In my father's case, though, more often than not it was a 'Yes, that'll be a 614432' or whatever, followed by a short walk to the bin where the part was stored. It was a rare gift which delighted his customers and sometimes amazed his peers.

Yet in his early married life, when presented with the opportunity to take over a spare parts agency in Ararat, he'd had difficulty in accepting the responsibility and failed the test. For his part I never heard him mention Ararat and not even my mother would talk much about it, just the occasional reference to his inability to pay enough attention to the books, whatever that meant. Maybe it was this difficulty which brought out his later tendency to blame a lack of progress or promotion at Preston Motors on everything from the influence of the Masons to incompetent bosses who failed to recognise his value—anything but sheet the blame home to himself.

It was as if anything was possible for my father, as long as it was in short bursts, as in the case of the taxi where, doubtless, his love of cars and driving had made it work for him, and he showed genuine pride when the money started to come in. But gradually he'd begun to regard it as a chore that got in the way of other things.

Such contradictions were also evident when it came to relationships. There is little doubt that his views had been shaped, at least in part, by growing up as one of nine boys, in a man's world where the men worked, played football and drank with other men while the wives looked after the home and children and cooked the meals.

In a social environment, like in a hotel lounge with friends, he appeared to 'wear' my mother with pride, as if her good looks and gentle shyness helped make his own presence more attractive. While there was no doubting his affection for her, when it came to my mother as an individual the contrast came out. If it appeared she was becoming the centre of attention, his mood would change quite suddenly, not enough to be detected by most but certainly by those who knew him well. My mother would see the signs of this change and gradually withdraw from the conversation, and it would soon be time to leave.

Once at home, he would use any pretext to start an argument with my mother. When she rose to the bait he would end it by accusing her of flirting with someone in the group. She had no answer to this and the arguments went nowhere, but at least they were predictable.

Certainly, there was a jealous streak in my father but it appeared more the case that he was unable to accept my mother might be a person in her own right, not merely a support mechanism for him. Perhaps as a result of this, my mother had few long-term friends; those who wished to be there for the long haul had to be strong and loyal enough to withstand my father's sarcastic asides, which he would occasionally use to deter them from encouraging her towards enjoying a life of her own.

Once, her oldest friend in Holbrook, Gwen Griffith, talked my mother into taking up golf—in many ways, Gwen Griffith and golf were just what my mother needed. Gwen and her husband John had a soldier–settler block called Boortkoi, just down the road from Jock Hulme's property Ardrossan. A tall, imposing woman, Gwen had an independent streak and quickly detected my father's selfishness when it came to my mother. She refused to be intimidated by him.

A keen golfer herself, Gwen insisted it would be the perfect outlet for my mother—one afternoon a week playing in the Holbrook Golf Club Associates competition and a few drinks with the other ladies afterwards would break the fourteen-hour days the café demanded. So my mother arranged to hire someone part-time for one afternoon a week and she and Gwen would head off to golf.

It wasn't long, however, before my father's annoyance at her absence became so obvious that even Gwen Griffith, with all her toughness, finally gave in to the belief that my mother continuing to play was only making her life more difficult. The whole issue must have been awkward for Gwen to understand, as she would have known only too well that my mother's half day a week on the golf course in no way impacted on my father's normal routine at the RSL.

Once my mother stopped playing her and my father's relationship, such as it was, returned to normal. Yet this lack of consideration for those closest to him could somehow spin in the reverse direction under some circumstances, and he was capable of going to extreme lengths to defend what might be regarded as family honour, even if it meant confronting entrenched family beliefs.

My father had grown up a Catholic, with that mix of loyalty and slight fear about things to do with the church, although he never had enough of either to be a regular churchgoer, while several of his former Catholic-school mates would eventually become priests at Albury's St Patrick's Church. So there was never any question that the first school I would attend while growing up in Albury, in the years before Holbrook, would be the Christian Brother's College, just over the road from St Pat's.

The college, or CBC, was a two-storey, red brick building with high-ceilinged classrooms which should have been light and airy but remained dark, due to deep brown wood panelling running halfway up the walls. Outside, a dirt playground offered little else beyond a handball court, mainly used by the Brothers themselves, which separated the main school building from the Brothers' residence at the eastern end of the school yard.

The Christian Brothers were the next step down in God's pecking order from the priests over the road at St Pat's and I can't remember any of them smiling much, maybe because they hadn't made it through the exam you needed to handle the bread and water at St Pat's each Sunday. They were at St Pat's every Sunday though, sitting in the pews up the front, always with their heads bowed and their eyes half closed; I often wondered whether that was because they were concentrating on explaining to God why they were so quick to reach for the cane.

Not everyone at CBC got the cane, especially if you were a favourite of the Brother who taught my class, a pudgy-faced man not much taller than my father with hair parted down the middle and with red-rimmed eyes that looked like he'd been up all night reading the Bible under a bad light. Being one of his favourites meant you got more attention than anyone else. Once he was finished giving lessons from the front of the classroom he would go with his favourite boy to the back of the room where the last row of seats was always vacant. There, you could hear him talking in a low voice as he helped his favourite with his lessons.

There were two doors at the side of our classroom, one at the front and one at the back, and both opened out into the passageway between our room and the other class-rooms at CBC. If you needed to go to the toilet you went out the front door to the right of the blackboard—that was the nearest to the toilet at the far end of the passageway—and you came back the same way.

Well, that was how it usually worked, until the morning I was coming back from the toilet and one of the other Brothers stopped me in the corridor. He asked me to take a box of chalk to a class at the far end of the passageway, beyond our own room. That was how I came to be entering our classroom from what was to turn out to be the wrong door, the one directly opposite the last row in the classroom.

I must have opened the door very quietly, because the instant I walked through the door I saw the Brother, who was sitting on the far side of the boy, pull his hand away from the front of the boy's pants. For a second or two I didn't recognise what I was seeing but then it became obvious. I turned my head away quickly and continued walking towards my seat up the front, but I could feel the heat rising in my face and turning it crimson red, so it seemed to be telling everyone in the class what I had seen.

Gradually the redness in my face subsided but some-how it still felt as if the Brother's eyes were burning into the back of my neck. While I tried to concentrate on my work, my mind was in turmoil as I attempted to work out what I would say if he asked me anything when he walked back to the front of the room.

But when he did walk back to the blackboard he said

nothing, and as the day went on he never once looked directly at me.

I could not get it out of my mind that night and although I desperately wanted to tell my mother I somehow felt too ashamed to try to describe what I had seen. Instead, I just began to hope that something would happen so that I would miss school the next day. As it turned out, it was as if nothing had happened and the Brother hardly looked at me all morning; by lunchtime I was starting to feel that nothing had really happened and anyway, if it had, it had all gone away.

As the end of the school day approached, the Brother left the room for a few minutes and when he returned he walked briskly to his desk in front of the blackboard and announced that an expensive fountain pen belonging to someone in the class had gone missing. Then, looking straight at me for the first time all day, he told me to come to the front of the class.

It seemed like my legs weren't part of me as I rose from my desk and walked towards the small stage at the front. Even before I reached it his voice seemed to boom at me as if it was coming from somewhere miles away outside the room.

'Jim Eames,' he said, 'I know you have taken it. I want you to bring it back tomorrow or you will no longer be able to come to this school. We don't want thieves among us.'

Then he told me to go home.

At first I just felt relief to be out of the classroom and away from that booming voice and all the stares, but when

I was on my own it seemed to be worse, my mind a strange jumble of guilt and confusion. By the time I had walked home I had long surrendered to tears, to such an extent that I could no longer keep it from my mother.

After I had told her several times I hadn't stolen the pen she must have started to doubt I was telling the truth, because she kept asking me over and over what was wrong.

'If you didn't steal the pen then you haven't got anything to worry about, so why are you still carrying on like this?' she asked me.

But how could I tell her about the other problem, about the Brother and the boy at the back of the class? How could I describe that to my mother?

Then she stopped her questioning. 'Well,' she concluded, 'you'll just have to wait until your father comes home.'

My mother must have sent a message to my father at work, because I'd never seen him come home so early before. Usually, he went straight to McLennan's Hotel after work and it wasn't until after dark that you would hear the rattle of his bike's mudguard as it bounced along the rough gravel path at the side of our house. This day however, it was still light when the rattling started, to be followed by that final thud of the handlebars against the back wall of the sleep-out. There were a few moments of whispered conversation between him and my mother and then he called me into their bedroom. As I entered, my mother left, as if she didn't want to be there when the execution took place. My father was sitting on the edge of their double bed, a cigarette in his hand as usual but his face expressionless as he tapped the bed beside him, indicating to me to sit. Without looking at me directly but staring ahead at the window, the interrogation started.

'Did you do it?'

'No.'

'Are you telling the truth?'

'Yes.'

'Why are you so upset if you're telling the truth?'

'I don't know.'

By now I was just managing to hold back tears.

By the time this process had been repeated three or four times, with the same questions and the same answers, and now fearing my father didn't believe me either, I could hold back the tears no longer and along with them came the whole story of the boy at the back of the class and the agony of the past two days.

When I had finished my father continued to sit there for what seemed like ages, though it was probably less than a minute, saying nothing, just continuing to stare out the window.

Then, suddenly, he stood up, took me firmly by the arm and said, 'Get your jumper. Get your jumper, we're going up to school.'

My mother was standing at the kitchen bench when we walked through, but he said nothing to her and she must have been wondering what was going on. Maybe she thought he was going to take me out and shoot me like he had our black kelpie bitch when she kept getting on heat.

When I looked back from near the sleep-out she was still standing there with a quizzical look on her face.

Dad said nothing more to me either as, with me propped on the handlebars with both legs dangling either side of the front wheel, he pedalled in silence the four blocks to CBC. Once there he leaned the bike against the red brick wall next to the school gate, told me to stay with it and walked off across the schoolyard towards the Brothers' residence.

It was almost dark by the time he returned. Although I could sense there was still anger in his voice when he told me to get back on the handlebars, I could somehow tell he was not annoyed with me anymore.

We rode home in silence and he never said another word to me about the incident. But I heard him tell my mother that night that he'd 'sorted them out'—whatever that meant.

My mother kept me home from school the next day, and when the time came for me to return the following day I dreaded what was going to happen when the lessons started. Just before playlunch, the Brother announced that the missing fountain pen had been found in the corner of its owner's schoolbag so everything was now back to normal. Several weeks went by and another Brother started taking our class—we never saw the old Brother again.

So somehow, when the threat of an injustice or a challenge was there, my father had no hesitation in rising to meet it, often with a degree of commitment which would surprise those who thought they knew him well.

In a way too, his venture into undertaking was nothing less than a leap of faith as he must have realised from the outset that, along with the more benign deaths by natural causes, there would come the shattered bodies and gruesome images from which nightmares are made.

24

The violent town

We'd only just sat down to dinner the night of Eulenstein's explosion and it shook the front window and rattled the crockery in the cupboard on the kitchen wall. My father thought at first the crash came from a head-on collision outside in the main street, and shouted something about calling an ambulance as he ran out onto the footpath.

But there was no sign of a crash, just the glow of flames and smoke rising from the east side of the highway a quarter of a mile north up the main street, just about where Eulenstein's garage was.

The flames weren't rising high at first but they must have been high enough to tell my father something pretty serious had happened. He ran towards the A70, and as he drove off there was a brief flare of light as a ball of flame wobbled its way out of the front of the building and onto the edge of the footpath where it stopped, giving off a faint glow. By now there were screams and shouting as shadowy figures, framed against the half light and the flames, could be seen running across the highway towards the building.

Only later when my father returned home would we learn that the brief fireball we had seen come to a stop on the road verge was the human torch of Melbourne transport driver Tim Dacyk, his clothes alight, crashing through the front plate-glass window of the garage and out onto the street. What we could not see was the other side of the horror taking place near the back of the garage. There, Dacyk's co-driver, Robert Jarvie, and the garage owner, Eric Eulenstein, clothes also alight, had both staggered out onto the side street.

By the time my father reached the scene someone was attempting to put out the flames engulfing one of the men with a bag, but his flesh kept coming off. The flames were finally snuffed out by wrapping him in a blanket. They pushed the screaming Jarvie to the ground and rolled him over to extinguish him.

By now the blue-tinged flames from the oxyacetylene cylinder Eric Eulenstein had been using were searing high into the building's roof and had set the rafters alight. But as luck would have it, Col Black, one of my father's premiership team, and the rest of the Holbrook Fire Brigade had been in the middle of their fortnightly fire drill just down the road in Young Street when the explosion went up. Like most of the rest of the town, they'd heard the explosion and saw the smoke and were on the scene in minutes.

There was nothing much the fire brigade could do to help the three victims. Their first concern was to stop the flames from the oxyacetylene cylinder setting fire to the whole building, but it was too hot and dangerous for anyone to approach with a foam extinguisher. Someone had the bright idea of throwing a rope around the cylinder and it was dragged outside so they could get at the flames engulfing the ceiling.

Later, a shocked Holbrook would learn that Jarvie and Dacyk had been travelling between Sydney and Melbourne when they'd noticed a leak in their furniture van's fuel tank and had stopped at Eulenstein's to have it repaired.

No one would ever know for certain whether the explosion had occurred because the tank had not been drained properly or even if the tank's cap had been left on when Eric Eulenstein started to weld the fracture causing the leak. But with Eulenstein bending over the tank and the other two standing nearby they had little chance when the tank exploded.

Eric Eulenstein died that night and Jarvie and Dacyk died in Albury Hospital early the next morning.

It was after 9 p.m. by the time we heard the car pull up out the front and my father came back into the kitchen. His face was white and he muttered something about someone trying to put out a burning body by beating it with a hessian bag, the burning flesh coming off. Then he turned and walked out into the backyard and there was silence for a few seconds. Then we heard him vomiting into the garden.

The Eulenstein explosion seemed to mark the high point of a period of exceptional disasters. It was hard to see why a country town that was no different to so many others deserved such an unfortunate reputation. Sure, there were no big-city type murders or matters of heavy criminal intent but nonetheless a succession of occurrences took place which brought with them devastation, death and destruction well beyond that normally to be expected in a community of 1400 people.

For a time it appeared there was little respite, as for three or four years violent death stalked the township and became almost a monthly occurrence. It wasn't just the people of Holbrook who noticed it—the town's reputation spread far beyond its borders, thanks in large part to the one common denominator which seemed to feature in most of them. The Hume Highway.

That crumbling ribbon of bitumen, which not only split the town in two but soaked itself in the blood of through-travellers and locals alike, had no worse section than the eighty-odd miles covering the stretch between Albury and Tarcutta. In time, this stretch began to be referred to in newspapers and on radio in Sydney and Melbourne as 'The Horror Stretch'. And, as the halfway point of the eighty miles, Holbrook was right in the middle of it all, as if it was going out of its way to earn a reputation.

Nothing appeared to be able to halt the horrors, each one having its own setting. There was the semitrailer that, in a fateful split second, broke away from its prime mover as it travelled downhill near the Wagga turnoff north of the town. It veered to the other side of the road, taking off the top of a Jaguar sedan coming in the opposite direction and decapitating its five occupants. There was the burning cattle truck that slammed into a tree on the roadside near the Woomargama Gap, incinerating the driver and his passenger and half the cattle in the back, and leaving the lingering stench of burnt flesh in the air for days.

Then there were the three Melbourne youngsters killed instantly when their Holden was split wide open in a head-on collision with a transport truck only a few hundred yards from where the blackened tree marked the cattle truck accident. It happened late in the morning and blocked part of the road so that every passing motorist couldn't help but see the prostrate bodies, half covered by blankets, stretched across the crumpled interior of the sedan.

And, although it wasn't really the job of the country undertaker, who else appeared better able to assist an ambulance driver in such cases? As with Eric Eulenstein, if there was a local involved it would make it worse for my father.

Then there was Jack Craig. Like most in town, Dad knew and liked young Jack Craig and occasionally even lightheartedly cautioned him about riding his motorcycle too fast. It was fatherly-type advice, as he'd had a Matchless motorbike similar to Jack's in his own youth. But Jack would just laugh and couldn't be expected to take much notice.

The police suspected the headlight on the Matchless failed as Jack approached a sweeping left-hander about three miles out of town at around nine o'clock on that Sunday night. My father had been one of the first there after a passing motorist raised the alarm. Jack's Matchless had just happened to leave the road dead in line with a corner post on the fenceline. The impact hurled his body along the top strand of barbed wire for thirty feet or so with such force that he partially dislodged two of the fence posts.

The bike's speedo had jammed at ninety-four miles per hour and when the police measured the distance between where the bike had become airborne and where it had finally landed, they found the machine had only hit the ground twice in 147 feet.

My father vomited into the garden that night too.

They didn't have to call Dad the night Len Wornes died. Len was the patriarch of the Wornes family and several of his sons had played or trained with the Mick Eames premiership team, while the rest of the family popped up somewhere in just about every sport in town.

Once again it would be the highway that would snatch life from Holbrook, and once again fate would take the country undertaker there within minutes of it happening.

Dad had taken my younger brother Pete with him to Albury on a taxi job when, not far from Table Top, the car's headlights picked up something unusual on the road ahead. By the time my father had got to within a hundred yards or so there was no longer anything unusual about it— the lights fell on crumpled metal and a whisp of steam rising from a shattered car radiator. He told Pete to stay in the car, that he'd 'sort it out'. But there was nothing he could do to help Len Wornes, Charlie Lugg or Les Parker. They'd died instantly as their Hudson slammed into the rear trailer of a semi.

They would not be the first or the last to die in this fashion, the victims perhaps of drivers blinded by oncoming headlights, unable to see a semitrailer parked on the side of the road.

The combination of these horrific events gradually began to take its toll on my father. The effect on him first became apparent when his drinking habits began to change. Soon, instead of a seven-ounce glass of beer forming the focal point of his drinking session at the RSL or his call at George Ross's Mullengandra pub, the first order would be: 'Just a scotch thanks, and not too much water.'

Something else changed, too. He became obsessive about teaching me to drive.

25

The driving instructor

I'm sure it was the carnage on the highway, and his close involvement with it, which convinced my father that the only way for me to stay alive on the road was for him to be ruthless in hammering home the dangers that lurked there.

Not that teaching me to drive was anything new. Much to the consternation of my mother, he'd jammed me beside him as soon as I was tall enough to see over the steering wheel—with the help of a padded cushion on the front seat. Of course, there was no hope of me reaching the pedals, but I could steer by reaching across in front of him while he rested his hands on his knees, ready to take control if something went wrong. It was awkward but I loved it and even became disappointed if a trip in the car went by without the offer to slide across alongside him and take the wheel.

My father seemed to enjoy it too, and his instructions were issued in a quiet, even tone, with just a hint of pride, as if he was relishing the possibility of someone aspiring to his own high standards which, he obviously believed (with the exception perhaps of his brother George's) were in a class of their own.

The fact that the change in his approach to teaching me to drive coincided with his sliding into even heavier drinking habits wasn't particularly noticeable at first. As time went on, the after-effects of the switch from beer to scotch during the customary pub stops began to mean that, now tall enough to see over the steering wheel and reach the pedals, I was—although well under licence age—spending more and more time behind the wheel.

But despite its increasing frequency, there was never anything structured about it. You could never accuse my father of sitting his teenaged son behind the wheel and going through what would normally be regarded as a formal driving lesson. Instead, typically, he would emerge into the darkness from the front door of the Mullengandra Hotel, walk to the passenger's side and announce gruffly, as if I should have anticipated it, 'You drive. And don't forget a thing I've told you.'

Thus, quite suddenly really, learning to drive was no longer fun but a deadly serious business. It could happen at any time of the day or night, but mostly at night, because it suited my father's drinking habits and also because he was convinced it was then that the highway was at its most lethal.

In some respects, there was a pattern to our 'lessons'. During the first few miles my father would repeat over and over again his mantra that good driving hinged on two basic attributes: good judgement and common sense. With those in your driving armoury, he would insist, you could handle any situation you might encounter on the road.

As we drove on in silence I'd remind myself of the other things he'd said: the car was never to be regarded as simply something that carried you from A to B—it should be something you wrapped around you and became one with. You just didn't drive it, you felt its every move and listened to it breathe with the aim of achieving some sort of harmony with it. Its engine was never to be unnecessarily strained, as this was regarded as nothing less than a form of abuse. Looking after it ensured you would be able to call on it for something extra in an emergency, because you should always be aware that acceleration was often more important than braking. Too few drivers, he would say, were aware that application of power at the right time could just as easily avoid trouble as excessive braking.

'You won't learn that at a city driving school,' he would say derisively, as if he was convinced that anyone who hadn't learnt to drive on a country road hadn't really learnt to drive. Properly judging your speed and its relationship to road conditions meant you could avoid using your brakes until you absolutely needed them and anyway, according to my father, anyone who was hard on brakes certainly would never be a good driver.

Such beliefs inevitably led to some unique instruction techniques. For instance, aware that the road for a few miles ahead involved a series of bends of varying degrees, my father would direct that you pass through the section at normal driving speed but without touching the brake, thus forcing you to accurately judge your approach speed to each corner so you could execute it smoothly, neither too fast nor too slow. The corners themselves were a whole new field for me. Every corner had its 'line', a path through it which offered the smoothest entry and exit and least strain on the vehicle.

Racing drivers like his friend Frank Kleinig never go around a corner, he would say, but straighten it out. Therefore, if the road was clear ahead you would cross partly onto the other side as you took a right-hander, based on the premise that if you had all the road, then you used it.

As for the car's speedometer, to my father it was an instrument of very limited use, little more than a decoration to encourage people not to exceed the speed limit in built-up areas. Any good driver should know within a mile per hour or so what speed he was doing at any given time, and that came from experience. The speedo meant little because your speed was directly related to how the car handled the road conditions and the numbers on the speedo's dial couldn't help you much there.

Nevertheless, he had a simple method of ensuring I wasn't tempted to rely on the speedo itself. He would first insist that, partly to overcome the glare factor while driving at night, all instrument lights in the vehicle be turned off. Sometimes, if the session at George's Ross's had been a particularly long one he would slip off into an alcohol-induced sleep and peace would reign as I pressed on along the highway.

Abruptly, the silence would be shattered. 'What speed are you doing now?' he'd ask me.

Being off the mark by five miles per hour or so, authenticated by turning on the lights to check the speedo, would result in a blast of invective which gradually subsided as he dropped off to sleep again.

There were other rules you disregarded at your peril and they usually revolved around my father's belief that every other driver on the road must be regarded as an idiot. That's why you never took your eys off an approaching car, in the belief that you were expecting the driver to do something stupid at the last second, like suddenly veer onto your side of the road. In that case your reaction must be instinctive as you must do anything to avoid a head-on collision, even if it meant leaving the road and hitting a tree. 'A tree's always a better bet,' he would say, 'because at least it's stationary and you have a better chance of survival.'

But it was the trucks my father regarded as the main enemy, the giant Internationals, Macks and Whites which totally occupied their side of the road and brushed you by inches as they passed. There were other trucks too, standing still on the side of the highway at night. They were every bit as lethal as those coming at you at a closing more than a hundred miles per hour.

If log books existed then they were honoured in the breach, as many truck drivers simply pressed on until they could go no further and pulled to a stop on the side of the road, occasionally with their unlit trailer at the very edge of the bitumen. 'So you must learn,' Dad would say, 'to keep one eye peeled for any dark shape which may be waiting to claim you on the side of the road, particularly when you're staring into the lights of an oncoming car.'

I don't think my father, despite all else he had seen, ever forgot that night when Len Wornes died. He figured too many people had paid the price for a truck driver's tiredness on Holbrook's Horror Stretch.

26

The big fire

Kelly O'Brien's mate Gordon McLaurin had seen the ominous signs long before that Wednesday in January. Out at Dalriada, north along the highway, Gordon and his father James had watched as a bumper spring delivered a luxurious carpet of grassland. But when the spring was over there had been no rain at all and the whole district was gradually transformed into a dull yellow tinge of cover which was so dry it crackled under foot.

Gordon and many others would ask the question repeatedly later, but by then it was too late. Why in God's name would a bunch of railway fettlers choose that time to start a burn-off operation near the railway line at Mangoplah?

First it got away into a grass fire which local firefighters managed to control, but in the searing 108-degree heat of that Wednesday it broke out again and this time they had no hope of stopping it.

You often hear radio reports of how winds fan a fire but that's only partly true. Bushfires don't need much outside help. They create their own wind and determine their own speed and direction and while you can backburn and mess about at the edges that's no use with a big one.

The *Border Morning Mail* would quickly label it the Red Terror, while Jock Hulme described it as a holocaust. To Col Black, sitting on the back of Holbrook's vintage fire truck, it was a snake. Like a big brown, it had waited for just the right time to strike, with a thirty-knot wind, foot-high grasses and little water in the dams with which to fight back.

Looking back years later, in these times when radio-controlled fire units are alerted to fresh outbreaks in minutes and aircraft dump tons of water on hot spots, it's hard to imagine the hopelessness of it all. In fact, at first nobody even knew it was coming.

It was around midday on the Thursday and Gordon had been out in the yards at Dalriada all morning drenching stock, when he noticed smoke on the horizon to the north-west. He called for his father to have a look.

James McLaurin had experienced enough fires in his years of farming to react instantly: 'Get back on your horse and start mustering. It'll be here tonight.'

Gordon didn't believe him. 'Oh come on Dad,' he replied. 'It's miles away.' But he did what he was told and headed off to round up the sheep and cattle.

By mid afternoon, billowing smoke curled across the horizon to the north of the town. But even though the police had sent Sergeant Joe Hawkins over from Wagga to coordinate operations, there was no real concern as far as the town itself was concerned as the north-westerly was sliding it away towards the east. Still, Col Black and the other eight members of the town's brigade had the 1928 red Garford out ready just in case they were needed, though they hoped it wasn't required to get anywhere fast.

The Garford always generated a laugh or two, particularly when it had to respond to anything at the northern end of the town where the main street had a slight uphill gradient. Not much, mind you, but enough to have Col and the other men on the back watch the local kids wave as they passed the Garford on their pushbikes.

Most people seemed pretty happy to have Joe Hawkins back in charge of operations at Holbrook, even my father, who always described Joe as a 'good copper' though he must have been still a bit cranky about losing his war with Len Condon over who should be picking up taxi fares on Holbrook's main street. He went off to see Joe Hawkins early that afternoon to see if he could help. Joe suggested he might be able to use cars like the A70 Austin later to take supplies out to some of the firefighters.

When Joe rang later in the afternoon he said they expected the wind to drop as it always did around sunset, and they might need some help out at Aberfeldie, a property just over the road from McLaurin's at Dalriada. Everyone hoped they'd stop the fire at the highway.

There wasn't much of a sunset that day as the smoke from the fire spread wider on the wind. As night came, you could see the glow of the fires to the north-west for the first time, but they still looked a long way away.

I was really excited when my father said I could go with him to Aberfeldie, as I figured I would be one of the few kids in town to get a chance to see this big fire first-hand. When my mother objected, she and my father started to argue, but he told her the experience would be good for me and he might also need some help when he got there, which I interpreted to mean that if he had some gates to open on the way into the property then I could do it. If there was one thing my father hated about driving a taxi in the country it was the requirement to get out of the car to open the sometimes two or three gates which separated the paddocks on most of the rural properties in the district. Besides, he told her, Joe Hawkins had said the fire was burning the other way so there was no chance we'd be too close to it, and the sandwiches and cordial on the back seat were for the firefighters who'd gathered at Aberfeldie before heading for the confrontation on the highway. We'd be coming straight back for more supplies.

I don't know whether any of that was true but my father must have been more concerned by the time we approached the meeting point at the back of Aberfeldie station. As we drove along the two-wheel track towards the last gate into the homestead paddock, the whole night sky half a mile away was ablaze and we seemed to have arrived just in time. It was obvious the small group of firefighters were already starting to move out, making shadowy outlines against the glow to the north as they ran from truck to truck throwing up knapsacks and bags and then jumping on themselves.

My father opened the back door and began handing out the cartons full of sandwiches and cordial, and I heard someone shout that the wind had changed and we should follow the two-wheel track straight ahead as it looped back to the highway. Then the trucks were gone.

We must have been heading towards the south-east because for a time the track went away at right angles to the fire, but then suddenly a blaze broke out to our right, about half a mile away, and was travelling in the same direction as us. By the time I had opened another gate it was outpacing us and Dad shouted to me to leave the gate open—he must have realised that if the fire reached the highway before us it would cut the road between us and Holbrook.

By now, visibility was cut to only a few yards and we almost crashed into the last gate as it suddenly appeared in front of us out of the smoke. As I ran to open it I could see that not only had the fire beaten us to the highway but the grass was alight a short distance away, meaning the fire had cut the highway on both sides of us. Then suddenly the A70 was on the bitumen surface again and it would only be later that I would realise how difficult my father's next decision must have been. His natural instinct must have been to turn right towards Holbrook and home. There was never any way of telling what my father thought during those moments; whether he had made the right choice of direction, or even whether he was now questioning the wisdom of bringing me along. You never could tell by looking at his face because his face never gave anything away. The most you got was that furrowed, determined look like it had had that afternoon when I sat on his bicycle as we headed towards his confrontation with the Christian Brothers at school.

Now, the main task was to stay on the bitumen because to leave it could mean hitting a guide post or fallen tree branch. But this was easier said than done as the smoke blanketed everything within a few yards of the car—everything except the fire, that is.

I looked across and could tell my father was concentrating hard, as he was crouching forward, peering ahead, and his hands gripped the wheel so tightly I thought he might break it. Because he'd made scores of trips to Aberfeldie before he would have known that the section of highway we were on now was straight for at least half a mile so if he could stay on the main road surface we might make it through, provided, of course, the car itself didn't catch alight.

Up until now he had said nothing since he'd told me back at Aberfieldie to leave the gate open, but there was even more tension in his voice when he next spoke. 'Tell me if you hear us leave the bitumen,' he instructed.

Normally, staying on the bitumen would have been relatively easy. Even if you couldn't see what was happening, you'd hear the change in tyre noise as the tyres left the smoothness of the tarred surface and crunched onto the gravel. But by now the sound of the fire itself was blotting out all other sounds and its noise was all around us.

Every few seconds amidst the rich red, a burst of white flame would momentarily turn the black smoke to grey as the top of a tree exploded, creating a ball of flame and myriad sparks both in front of and above us. Then there would be a whooshing sound as the fireball gathered up its embers and was carried off by the wind, setting alight other trees as it went.

It must have been one of those brief split seconds of light which saved Doug Young's life because suddenly the car had stopped and my father was shouting out the window on his side, 'Here. Over here!'

It was then I saw the hunched figure for the first time as it lurched towards us out of the smoke, hesitating for a second as if unsure of the direction my father's shout had come from. Then, handkerchief clutched to his face and coughing uncontrollably, Senior Constable Doug Young staggered the last few steps towards the car. By the time he reached us my father had the back door open and Doug fell across the back seat, still coughing. There was another rush of hot air and smoke as my father opened his own door again, then he was back behind the wheel and we were moving.

The driving was getting easier now as visibility improved through the smoke ahead. Fortunately for us, the sheer speed of the fire had treated the natural firebreak of the highway with contempt and had flashed across it in a matter of minutes. Although there were still burning trees and fence posts on either side, the fireballs and their whooshing sounds which marked the main front of the blaze were now behind us.

We were well clear when my father stopped again to check the car, and it was then that Doug Young explained he'd been heading to Aberfeldie on the police motorcycle when, like us, he suddenly found himself surrounded by fire as it jumped the road. Blinded by the smoke, he must have left the bitumen because the next thing he remembered was the motorcycle's sidecar colliding with something hard. He was tossed off and found himself stumbling around amid the flames and smoke.

Not knowing which way to walk or run and fast becoming overcome by smoke, he was on his last legs when he heard my father shout and could just see the glow of the A70's headlights a few yards away.

'If you hadn't come along Mick, I reckon I was a goner,' he told my father.

As we drove back into Holbrook we could see there was no longer any doubt that the town was fearing the worst. We stopped briefly alongside the Holbrook brigade's old Garford, which was working hard filling its water tanks from the town's mains. Col Black told my father the wind had changed from the north-west to the north-east, swinging the fire back in the direction of the town. The brigade would make a stand at the town's northern edge. My father spent the next few hours that night joining other vehicles in evacuating families who lived on the edge of town to the showgrounds and the shire hall.

And they did make their stand north of the town early the next morning. But no one who fought the blaze that night would take credit for saving Holbrook. Just as the fire front breasted a hill about a mile and a half from the town at around 1.30 a.m., the wind miraculously changed back to the north-west. The fire skirted the edge of town, heading south-east towards the Jingellic Road.

Holbrook was saved that night but not much else was. While my father had been trying to keep the A70 on the bitumen, a mile or so behind us Gordon McLaurin and his father James were battling to save Dalriada as the fire roared past them and across the highway. Gordon suffered third-degree burns but they'd managed to save the homestead and the shearers quarters although everything else was lost, along with eight hundred head of cattle and four thousand sheep. They saved the horses, though; Gordon had always insisted his draught horse Patch had more brains than the rest of his horses and Patch proved it that night. He kicked down the gate holding them in and led them all into the dam.

Gordon could hardly believe even a bushfire could create such intense heat. It was proved to him next morning, however, when he sifted through the remains of the equipment shed fifty yards from the house—the steel crowbar was one of the few items still recognisable, except the heat had reduced it to half its original size.

There were a lot of lucky people that night. One of them was Jock Hulme, who'd been fighting the fire not far from Gordon's place when someone told him it was heading towards his own property, Ardrossan, on Jingellic Road. Jock and a few who offered to help reached Ardrossan in time to try and clear a firebreak around the house, only to watch helplessly as the fire jumped the road and headed towards the homestead. Not only did they realise they wouldn't save the house, but if they didn't move quickly they'd go up with it. By the time they all reached Jock's truck and started the engine, the fire was all around them. The smoke was so thick they couldn't see much further than the end of the truck's bonnet.

Jock reckoned their only hope was to drive for the creek which ran a few hundred yards away from the house, but because of the smoke he could only hope he was heading in the right direction. He finally knew they'd arrived when the truck came to a sudden stop as its front wheels dropped over the creek's edge and jammed the chassis on the bank. The men ran the last few feet down into the creek and knelt in the water, splashing their faces as the fire seared over the top of them. Jock noticed that even though the creek was running, the water was warm.

When the fire passed and the smoke began to clear, Jock looked upon a still-smouldering landscape. The house was gone and along with it all the presents from his and his wife Shirley's wedding three months before. In fact, the only thing left standing were ten acres of dead timber, which told him something about the discriminatory habits of bushfires. In a way though, Jock was one of the lucky ones—only a few days before, he'd taken several thousand sheep to the sale yards in Albury.

No human effort stopped the Red Terror that summer, as it jumped the Murray River not far from Alf Wright's pub at Dora Dora and burned off into Victoria's timber country, finally being extinguished days later by heavy rains some-where towards the coast.

Holbrook licked its wounds as four hundred thousand acres of rich pastures resembled a blackened wasteland, dotted by the skeletal remains of numerous country home-steads and outbuildings.

In the days that followed, we sat on the kerbside outside Kane's Motors and watched as Joe Hawkins marshalled the scores of trucks arriving from far away carrying fodder for the surviving stock. Nace Kane hurried backwards and forwards to the shire office signing shooting permits. In the distance, you could hear the shots as the farmers with the permits put still-alive but often blinded or badly burned sheep out of their misery.

Doug Young told someone he was going to recommend my father for a medal but nothing came of it, probably because there were many other courageous things done that night and the next day.

My father next saw Doug when he called around the following night and said he needed the country undertaker to come with him to Lankey's Creek, out on the Jingellic Road, where they'd found the charred remains of Jesse Woodland lying in what was left of his hut.

Given the massive destruction wreaked by the Red Terror, my father would always be surprised there hadn't been more calls for the services of the country undertaker.

27

The end

I can't recall whether there was any specific moment when I realised my father was an alcoholic. Maybe that's because, in his case, there wasn't any particular happening or moment that marked it, but rather an increase in the behaviour and signs which had already been there for some time. Strangely though, it was to become easier for me to recognise due to the fact that I wasn't there.

Boarding school came out of the blue, partly because my father and Nace Kane had discussed it during one of their regular card games. Since Nace's son Peter had left Holbrook for Assumption College, Kilmore, the year before, the prospect of a good Catholic education with the Marist Brothers probably appealed to the conscience of a father who, despite for years not having been inside a Catholic church for anything other than his undertaking duties, somehow still leaned towards the values of a Catholic upbringing.

But if my father's motives were conscience-driven, it was not until much later I would discover the real reason my mother had agreed. Even then she must have been coming to recognise that my father's drinking and gambling habits would, should they worsen, eventually lead to difficulties in affording such things as sending her son three hundred miles away to boarding school. With the takings from the café already being bled to contribute to the upkeep of the taxi business, she had probably already concluded that it had better happen before the money ran out.

My parents argued often now about the funeral business, and you could tell from these arguments that my father had not bothered to heed Bill Lester's advice to 'get 'em while the tears are falling' when it came to being paid for funerals. While, as the shouting raged, he would take little notice when my mother repeatedly accused him of drinking and gambling too much, the arguments would reach a higher level when she questioned why it was mostly by the wealthier graziers that the majority of the money was owed. But while he would shout back at her that it wasn't his fault if people didn't pay, somehow I knew that the problem had more to do with a loss of face on his part should he be forced to ask for money from people above his social standing.

Whatever the reason I was sent to Kilmore, if there was to be a marker as to how difficult times had become it was on my first Christmas holiday home. The prospect of this holiday had started so well when, two weeks before the holidays were due to start, my mother had told me in a letter that I would not be coming home on the train to Albury as normal but my father would pick me up on his way home from Melbourne. It wasn't until he arrived at the college that morning that I saw the shiny new two-tone blue and grey Holden, delivered fresh that day from General Motors–Holden at Fishermen's Bend, and he proudly announced that the old A70 had gone. This was to be the new taxi.

It took us longer than normal to reach Holbrook that holiday, as there were the numerous hotel stops along the way, including a particularly long one at McLennan's Hotel where he kept taking people outside to show them the new addition to the Eames taxi business.

It wasn't until we reached Holbrook in the evening, however, that I realised my father's excitement and pride in the new arrival wasn't shared by my mother. Somehow she seemed to have got older in my absence and there was a tiredness in her voice which had not been there before. It was as if she'd given up trying to fight a losing battle against influences beyond her control.

It was the next morning, after my father had gone to the club, that she broke the news that the café would be sold. My father had taken little part in the decision, something I could understand as I always knew he resented the degree of independence the café gave her. And since she hadn't felt able to talk to him about it she'd talked to her friend Gwen Griffith, whom she often turned to when she needed support because Gwen, more than any of her friends, knew the reason for her problems. Gwen, she told me, had agreed she should sell while the business was still running and worth something rather than wait until it was unable to meet even its own expenses.

So, even before I left to return to school at the end of January, the café had been sold and my mother had agreed to work there for a time to help the new people settle in. Nothing much had changed for my father, though, who was still spending most of his time at the club with the shiny new Holden parked idly outside.

None of the letters from home that next school term ever referred to an increase in the problems, as that was not my mother's way, but rather they continued to talk about the little things that happened around the town, the contacts with her sisters, how Uncle George came out to stay for a few days and how he and my father talked endlessly about cars and driving, although not a mention that they probably did most of their talking at the RSL.

But not long after I arrived home for the Easter holidays I noticed something else had changed, and it wasn't for the better. Up till now, no matter how often and long he drank at the club or the Top Pub, my father would always come home for the evening meal, even though he would invariably return to the club after eating and not get home again until late that night. Now however, even though my mother would prepare his meal for him every night, it was often not until very late that he would arrive home and most times the meal would still be there uneaten the following morning.

As I lay in bed I could hear them arguing late into the night, on and on about money and drinking until his voice would fade away and he would go to sleep in the middle of an argument. Then there was a period of several days where we hardly saw him at all and when he did eventually arrive home he barely spoke and went straight to bed.

He didn't come out for breakfast the next day and it was late in the morning when my mother finally went into the bedroom to call him, as she wanted to make the bed. From the kitchen, I heard her talking at first, her voice strangely muffled, but then I realised that she was calling me to come quickly as if she didn't want anyone else to hear her.

When I walked into the bedroom she wasn't looking in my direction but sitting on the far side of the bed with her back to me, talking gently to my father who appeared to be in the strangest position. He was kneeling, resting back on his haunches in the middle of the bed like a small child waiting for someone to play with him. Although he looked up when I came into the room I could see no recognition in his eyes. Then he slowly lowered his head and, staring down at the bed immediately in front of him, began to run his fingers along the folds in the blanket as if looking for something. Back and forth his hands went, tracing the folds in the blanket, all the time his voice a low murmur as he kept repeating, 'Oysters. Where are the oysters? I can't find the oysters.' Over and over again he said it as his eyes followed the movement of his hands back and forth across the bed.

Then my mother spoke softly again as if he was still asleep and she didn't want to wake him, telling me to sit with him and keep talking while she called the doctor.

By the time the doctor arrived, my father had stopped looking for the oysters and was just sitting there in his pyjamas. The doctor gave him something to drink and gently eased him into a lying position under the blankets, then told my mother she should let him sleep.

And sleep he did. My mother kept going to the bedroom every hour or so to check on him, but I saw no more of him until late the following afternoon when he came and sat in a chair in the lounge room, a blanket wrapped around his shoulders. He didn't speak, just sat there staring at the empty fireplace, a faraway look in his eyes. Later that night he returned to bed.

The following day he dressed himself, but another day passed where he said very little, only nodding slightly to my mother when she gave him something to eat. In the days that followed, as he gradually improved, I asked my mother several times what was wrong with him but she would only say he was ill and change the subject. Then Gwen Griffith and her husband John called in, and while John was talking to my father in the lounge room, I heard my mother tell Gwen that he'd got something called 'the horrors' which the doctor said had been caused by alcohol and required days of rest.

As usual, between school holidays my mother never mentioned any more about such things in her letters to me at Kilmore, which still arrived religiously every fortnight. I could see though, during the holidays themselves, that my father had not changed his drinking habits. Despite that, there were still occasions when he insisted in putting me behind the wheel and repeating the mantra which he believed essential to keep you alive on the highway. Although failure might be beckoning in other parts of his life, I sensed there was no way it was going to intrude on the driving instructor.

But it was obvious too that my mother was finding it even harder to meet the fees necessary to keep me at Kilmore. With the taxi bleeding the money received from the sale of the café and a long time between funerals, it was hardly a surprise for Nace Kane when Mum told him I wouldn't be returning to Kilmore the next year.

My father seemed to take hardly any part in the decision, except to ask me whether I still wanted to be a journalist and if so he'd try to get me a job at the *Border Morning Mail* in Albury. He was true to his word, and due to his appeal to an old friend from his sporting days, I found myself hired as a cadet journalist with a weekly starting salary of six pounds one shilling and sixpence.

Sometime during the next year my father's pride and joy, the two-tone FJ Holden taxi, fell victim to his gradually diminishing income. It was replaced by an older second-hand model whose main role was to cover the three blocks between our house and the RSL. It had another function, though, one that once again would reveal that side of my father which, despite the grasp of alcohol and sliding self-esteem, would come to the fore where family was concerned.

Because of my meagre cadet journalist salary, I would often be forced to hitchhike the forty miles home to

Holbrook at weekends to save the additional cost of boarding for those two days in Albury. This meant I would have to return to Albury for a 3 p.m. start at the *Border Morning Mail* on the following Monday afternoon, and to achieve this deadline my father had developed a unique technique of his own.

About mid morning on the Monday, we would climb into the Holden and park on the roadside at the southern end of town, just short of where the town limits gave way to the highway in the direction of Albury. There we would wait for what he described as 'the right truck'. Ideally, the right truck meant a big red International of the type operated by Burmeisters Freight Lines. Somehow, in all his years traversing the Hume Highway, my father had come to the conclusion that the Burmeisters drivers were a notch above the others, so they were his preferred target.

'Here comes one now,' he'd say, as a Burmeisters road giant filled the rear view mirror of the Holden.

Once the semi had passed, the Holden would swing off in pursuit. Then as the truck left the town precincts my father would pull the Holden up alongside the truck's cab and, with a combination of horn sounding and hand signals, encourage the driver to pull over. He'd then explain that his son had to reach Albury by three o'clock that afternoon and that the Burmeisters people were the only ones he trusted.

It might have been unorthodox, but it never failed to result in the offer of a ride!

* *

One Thursday night my mother phoned me at work. I could sense the resignation in her voice when she explained she had had enough and that she and my brother Pete would be coming back to Albury to live, to our old house in Townsend Street. She needed me to come home that weekend and help pack. She said nothing about my father and what he thought about it but I knew by the emotion in her voice that she was close to tears, so it was better not to ask.

When I arrived in Holbrook the following night she told me she had arranged to borrow Gwen's husband's truck, and we would pack it next morning and I would drive it to Albury. It would all be done, she said, while my father was at the RSL.

At first I felt guilty at what we were doing behind his back, but the feeling didn't last long when I realised what the decision must have represented for a normally shy, retiring person like my mother. For her, not only must it have required determination and courage but she must also have been mindful of the shame and embarrassment she would feel when her Holbrook friends realised what had happened.

She must have been even more apprehensive about how my father would react but she showed no signs of it as we loaded the blunt-nosed Austin flat top with what furniture she considered essential. We were gone within an hour.

A strange quiet followed for almost two months. We heard nothing about my father and he made no effort to contact my mother. I think she began to settle into the belief that the trauma and struggle of the last few years was hopefully now behind her.

Once, she mentioned that she'd heard a funeral announcement over the radio for a burial at Holbrook which had been unusual in that the funeral had been conducted not by M. Eames, Funeral Director, Holbrook, but by his Culcairn counterpart. But she showed no interest in finding out the reason.

She settled in well to a job at Spalding's sandwich shop off Albury's main street and arranged for Pete to start at Albury Public School in David Street, only a few blocks from the Terminus Hotel. The sandwich shop job suited her well because most of the work involved catering for the lunchtime customers, which meant she could be home in time for Pete's return from school.

Then one day he didn't come home. First, she rode her bike to the school but one of the teachers told her he'd last seen my brother at the gate after school, so she came home again and waited. Although it was unlike him, she was hoping he had gone to someone else's place to play.

By the time darkness came my mother was on the edge of panic so she rode uptown again, this time to the Albury Police Station. The policeman said he would ring Holbrook. She waited for nearly an hour until word came that the policeman there had found my father at the Top Pub and my brother Pete was with him. He was safe and sound and eating a meal in the hotel kitchen. There was nothing the police could do, but they must have had some influence on my father because by the time school started two days later he'd dropped Pete off at the school gate.

On two more occasions in the months that followed my brother failed to arrive home from school as my father continued to take his revenge. Although by now she knew where to look, it must have worried my mother for numerous reasons, not least being her belief that my father was drinking heavily while driving the car. Still, the police were understanding and would always take the time to telephone Holbrook and confirm my brother was safe. As for Pete himself, such to-ing and fro-ing even had its moments of excitement; on one occasion he arrived home in a police car when the Holbrook policeman had somehow convinced my father he had to travel to Albury on a job and he'd drop Pete off on the way!

Then we lost contact with my father for several months, until one afternoon, not long after my mother had arrived home from work, a nursing sister from Albury Base Hospital came to the front door to tell her my father had been rushed to hospital. When my mother reached his bedside they told her he had a serious ulcer problem and had lost a great deal of blood. Two weeks later he was released with stern warnings not to drink, but my mother was sceptical of his ability to comply.

The two of them must have reached some agreement, because when he was released he came back to Albury to live. And it wasn't long afterwards that my mother broke the news to us that the funeral business would be sold. Even though it still owed my father money, it was obvious he could no longer run the business and the last chapter closed on my father's Holbrook years. Ironically, the man who purchased it was the ambulance driver with whom my father had shared numerous tragedies wrought by the killer highway over the years.

When his health improved to the point where he could work again, my father got a job for a time in the spare parts section of Wiltshire Motors. But that didn't last long after they found him making frequent trips down the street to Ryan's Hotel for what he called a 'few kickers' of whisky to get him through the day.

Then he got a job five miles away past Wodonga at Bandiana military base, re-fusing ammunition which he would occasionally delight in telling someone was being sent off to the islands north of Australia to discourage his old enemy 'Sockarino' from his designs on Borneo.

When he became ill again it initially looked like a serious bout of 'flu, but when my mother called the doctor he told them both that my father would have to stop drinking altogether or his liver would fail. He took the next day off work and my mother asked Nanna Eames to keep an eye on him while she went to work at Spaldings. So his own mother was with him when he took the turn but there was nothing she could do.

At the funeral, they talked a lot about his love of football and his talents as a spare parts man, but there was only a passing reference to his career as a country undertaker. I doubt that would have bothered him too much, however, as I never heard him mention anything about funerals after he came to live with us again in Albury. Maybe even the funny side of the business has its limitations when your memories are crowded out by too many gruesome images.

I thought of him, though, in the instant when Bill Lester's driver clashed the gears as the hearse negotiated the deep gutter outside St Patrick's Church that day. He would have had something to say about that from in the back.

I thought of my mother, too, when she realised we couldn't scrape up enough money for the funeral and she had to borrow the balance from Uncle Dave, the one she'd never forgiven for talking my father into an umpiring career. And it must have been especially hard for her to ride her bike up to his place at East Albury every month to pay him back.

Epilogue

Like much of country Australia, Holbrook has changed a lot since the 1950s. While the Hume Highway still splits it squarely in two, perhaps its most distinguishing mark now is the hull of an Oberon Class submarine, HMAS *Otway*, donated by the Royal Australian Navy in honour of the town's founder. Lt Commander Norman Holbrook would be pleased. Like the Woolpack Inn, the museum that occupies what was formerly the Bottom Pub, the *Otway* helps through-travellers visit the district's past.

The Ten Mile Creek still reverts to isolated water holes in summer, but it's of little consequence now as there's a modern swimming pool just down the road. The Shire Hall is still there, just as it was in those days, dominating the corner where the Hume Highway intersects with the road from Culcairn. If I look at it for long enough I can still sense the presence of Karly Bounader, that generous, gentle, giant of a man who brought the magic of movies even to those of us who often didn't have the extra sixpence to go upstairs. 'In you go,' he'd mutter, with a wry smile.

As for my father's watering holes: the remnants of a wooden tank-stand appear to be all that remains of the Billabong Pub, and George Ross's Mullengandra Hotel closed down some years back. It may be a private home now, but it looks exactly as it did in my father's day, its long, green roofed verandah still beckoning as you hurry past. The now silent wooden structure that was once the Dora Dora Pub still commands the high ground over-looking the Murray River at Talmalmo, but the pub itself no longer functions, apparently the casualty of a bitter family dispute over its future. If you peek through the front window of the bar you can see several examples of Alf Wright's memorabilia still tacked to the walls. Maybe they forgot to take them down.

As for the characters who made the town what it was . . .

My father's original Holbrook boss, Ignatius Patrick Kane, his best friend Jock Hulme and that man for all seasons, Sausage Jamison, have all passed on.

Kelly O'Brien, my father's gravedigger, remained a town identity until a stroke robbed him of his mobility and much of his speech, and therefore his most precious asset—his ability to communicate his unique earthiness and his devastating wit. His old mate Gordon McLaurin says Kelly found that hard to deal with in the years before his death at 79. It must have been doubly hard for an 'outside' man.

Gordon himself, now in his 80s, still tends to his stock at Dalriada, watching them graze across the same paddocks that saw the ravages of the 1952 fire. He describes the trip up the highway in the Essex as if it occurred only yesterday, although these days it's hard to recognize the Kyeamba Gap, now hardly a hump on the wide bitumen road.

Someone said the old Essex was spotted years later in Albury, its funereal accoutrements sacrificed to make way for the practicality of a ute. But no one knows what happened to my father's pride and joy, the 1938 8/90 Buick hearse. Not even the Albury funeral director who finally took over the business some years back can help there. It just disappeared.

Uncle Jack, now in his 80s, is the only surviving member of the nine Eames boys, none of his brothers making it to the age of 70. Talking to him seems to bring my father and Uncle George to life, and at the slightest prompting he'll recount the story of the day George fought the Alabama Kid.

As for George's driving prowess, a few years back, Jack and his wife Lois were travelling along the Mitta Mitta to Omeo road when the local chap driving the car pointed to a big ironbark off to the left and said proudly, 'That's George Eames' tree.'

'Yes, I know it well,' said Jack, the image still clear of his terrified brother Jeff staring over the edge from atop the timber jinker's load.

And as for my own father's driving ability and his somewhat unique driving instruction methods, they've saved my hide on the highway a hundred times in the years since.

After some years my mother married again and moved to the New South Wales South Coast, coming back to Albury only rarely. I don't think she ever returned to Holbrook for a visit. Perhaps she wanted to leave it all behind her, but in her shy, self-effacing way, she would have been surprised by the number of people there who remembered her fondly. Over time she gradually became more comfortable talking about what went on during those undertaking days and, although she sometimes appeared confused about what happened where, when and to whom, I hope I have managed to string it together as accurately as possible. Her last years were happy ones, seeing her grandchildren grow into adulthood, until she was forced to battle a blood disorder which finally claimed her in 1998.

If his 'kidnapping' and the other traumas of some of those years ever affected my brother Pete he's never shown it. In fact, he followed in our father's footsteps and is now one of the district's most respected spare parts managers, although he has never revealed any inclination to be an undertaker.

For my own part, I moved away to a career in journalism and for many years lost contact with my roots. Then one day I sat down to write a brief family history for our three children. It wasn't long before I began to realise I had embarked on a personal journey into the life of a father I had remembered mainly for his flaws. As the journey continued it began to reveal the character that existed alongside those flaws. And the more people I talked to about those days, the more I realised that he wasn't the only character in town—he was surrounded by them. Together they represented an era which no longer exists in Australia; the advances in communications and transport which started with the end of World War II along with the increasing pressures of daily life encouraged it to fade perhaps more quickly than it deserved.

In the end, however, it would be wrong to pass judgement on those days based on today's standards of political correctness. That was the way they were and that was the way it was, and I thank them all for the journey. I know they'd all agree if I said it's been a lot of fun and one helluva ride.

Acknowledgements

It was some years after my father's death that I came to the realisation that he had been such a normal part of the tapestry that represented country Australia in the post World War II years.

His kind were an unusual lot by today's standards, products of a male dominated society and certainly one where the term 'political correctness' had not been part of the vocabulary.

But in reality the only difference between Mick Eames and those who surrounded him was the fact that he had, for one period of his relatively short life, listed the occupation 'Funeral Director' behind his name. Beyond that they simply all inhabited an era in which there were no computers, it still took several days to get to London for those few who could afford it and the nearest thing to an automatic transmission was the 'Fluid Drive' mechanism on the 1948 Dodge.

In recapturing such times perhaps my greatest debt

to my father's younger brother Jack Eames. The only surviving member of the nine Eames boys he was able to recall aspects of my father's early life which were essential to understanding his character, and which otherwise would have been lost forever.

Others who helped paint the picture and to whom I am deeply indebted are Gordon McLaurin who so capably brought his old gravedigger mate Kelly O'Brien to life and my old friend Peter Kane whose father Nace, was initially my father's Holbrook boss. Sadly Peter was taken from us before work on this book was completed. Brian Brennan, George Cottrell and Tom Jones assisted me in filling in the football years while Jock Hulme and Colin Black were invaluable in describing the devastation of the bushfire of 1952.

Peter and Helen Meredith, Ray Stean, Frank and Pam Wornes, Len Condon, John Serong and Alan Bounader were generous with their time and memories and Arthur Larcombe was invaluable in capturing the atmosphere and the unique characters that made Holbrook such an memorable place to live in the late 40s and 1950s. Ivan Lyons, Mike Egan and Alan Henshaw added to my education on the business of undertaking and proved that, while the processes may have changed, country undertakers everywhere still bring a vibrant sense of humour to an otherwise serious profession.

There have been many others, too numerous to mention, who have provided essential ingredients to complete the whole. They know who they are and I owe them my thanks.

Lastly, it was the enthusiastic encouragement of Rebecca Kaiser of Allen and Unwin that lifted me over the final hurdle. It was then up to the steady hand of Karen Gee to sort out my split infinitives and to turn the raw prose into a book.

In the final analysis, however, none of it would have been possible without the unwavering support of my wife Jose who, at various times, filled the roles of research assistant, ideas factory and memory prodder and our children Steven, Suzanne and Frances. They never knew their grandfather but they insisted that was just another good reason why it should be written down. So too my brother Pete who relived some at times fragile memories with patience and good humour.

They'll be happy now. It's done.

Printed in Dunstable, United Kingdom